CHRISTIAN EDUCATION AND THE BIBLE

by

DOUGLAS S. HUBERY

General Secretary, Methodist Youth Department

CHESTER HOUSE PUBLICATIONS

2 CHESTER HOUSE, PAGES LANE, LONDON, N.10

First Published 1967

Made and printed in Great Britain by
Cox & Wyman Ltd., London, Reading and Fakenham
6250/67

ACKNOWLEDGMENTS

DURING the past ten years it has been my happy privilege to work in close association with Mr. Ernest Hayes. His contributions to Christian education as editor and author and administrator have become known throughout the world, and I have learned much from him. It is largely due to his persistence that this book has been written, and it is to him that it is now affectionately and respectfully dedicated.

Some parts of the early chapters of the book formed the basis of lectures given to students when I was Youth Tutor at Westhill College, Birmingham, and the questions raised in discussions and seminars helped me to clarify my own views. It will be apparent to all readers that I have been greatly influenced by the writings of Dr. R. J. Goldman and I am always glad to acknowledge my indebtedness to him. As colleagues together some years ago at Westhill we shared many experiments and began an unofficial dialogue in religious ideas which has continued ever since.

I am grateful, too, for the opportunity of discussing certain ideas contained in this book with my friend, the Rev. Rupert E. Davies, and would like in advance to exonerate him from any responsibility for lapses in historical accuracy, biblical interpretation or educational theory, even as I pay tribute to him for what I have learned from him.

DOUGLAS S. HUBERY

October 1966.

TO
ERNEST H. HAYES

CONTENTS

INTRODUCTION

THESE words are being written while I am on holiday in a mediaeval town built upon and into the rocks of the French Alps high above the Mediterranean Sea. The town has remained largely unchanged throughout its history, and while today there are modern roads leading to the coast, and one has the advantage of electricity and telephonic communication, its houses are the same as when they were built, the narrow cobbled alleyways and streets still run to the parapets, and the atmosphere is far removed from the commercialism and industrialization of a modern civilization. In its lifetime the town has witnessed the battles of the centuries on the high seas, in the valleys below, and among the surrounding hills. But it has itself been unmoved by them.

It is appropriate to write a book about the Bible in such an environment, for one is reminded inevitably that the Bible itself is very much like this town. Modern scholarship may bring new illumination and open up new lines of communication, yet as a book it remains much the same. Controversy and discussion, even hostility, may centre from time to time upon its pages. Yet it continues to endure. And whatever the readers of this publication may infer to be my own attitude towards the Bible, I can only assert that for me the more I am driven to its study the greater becomes my respect for its range of truth and breadth of vision. When every word has been spoken, the Scriptures remain 'profitable for teaching, for reproof, for correction, and for training in righteousness, that the man of God may be complete, equipped for every good work'.[1]

To begin with a personal testimony of this kind is not to shut one's eyes to the many problems associated with a proper understanding of the Bible. And for the teacher of the Christian religion, committed by his very vocation to the task of communicating God's truth as revealed in Scripture, those problems have to be resolved.

There is no need for me to emphasize that Christian education, to be effective, must be relevant in terms of life as it is lived today. My position in this regard has already been established.[2] However much one sees the need to be contemporary in these matters, it is nevertheless impossible to deal with the subject seriously without sooner or later having to come to terms with biblical records. It is not for nothing that the Christian faith is grounded in Bible history rather than in a series of abstract propositions. Even if the teacher may wish to avoid too strong an emphasis upon the Bible, or to skirt round its problems, his students or pupils will certainly have their questions to ask.

For some, of course, there is no embarrassment or inhibition in declaring God's truth as from the words of the Bible itself. These people have their own built-in attitude to the Bible as an infallible authority to be accepted without question. For them problems which seem to arise are conjured up in the minds of those who lack faith in God's ways with men. They are happy to ignore the problems, or to assume that they do not really exist, in the confidence that by so doing they are witnesses to the God they serve.

[1] 2 Timothy 3. 16.
[2] cf. my *Experiential Approach to Christian Education* (N.S.S.U.), 1960; and *Teaching the Christian Faith Today* (N.S.S.U.), 1964.

For others, the problems associated with the Bible are so many and so complicated that it becomes easier to proceed on the understanding that there is nothing special about the Bible, that it has its parallels in other religions, and that it should be regarded simply as one among many religious books to which reference may be made.

Between these extreme points of view there are many more educators and teachers who look for a synthesis. They are bewildered by some of the criticisms that seem to be raised against the Bible, and particularly at the present time they are concerned because it would appear that the Bible should not be taught to children. And their anxiety stems from a feeling which they cannot altogether rationalize that the Bible is different from other books and does have some kind of authority. At the same time they are ready to acknowledge that scientific knowledge has led to a changed attitude to the Bible, and their own honesty compels them to reject a Fundamentalist position.

If a synthesis is to be achieved, and a proper attitude to the Bible developed, it is essential to recognize at the very beginning that if God is the God of truth, then He is the God of all truth. It is fatal to compartmentalize one's thinking into separate categories. Over the centuries, and more particularly during the past one hundred and fifty years, the Bible has been subject to greater scrutiny and more intensive examination by scholars of all kinds than any other book that has been written. But while this analysis has been taking place, there have also been detailed researches into the psychology of human beings themselves with consequent illumination into the meaning of personality, capacity to learn, and the underlying causes of emotional and rational responses to the world and its relationships. The task of the teacher is not merely to synthesize knowledge of the Bible; he must also have the ability to relate this to himself as a person and at the same time to relate it to those whom he seeks to serve.

To attempt this kind of synthesis in a modest volume is perhaps to attempt the impossible. It is made, not because I believe I have anything original to contribute to the discussions on the Bible and Christian Education now being pursued at academic levels. It is made because I am only too well aware of the thousands of ordinary practitioners who are conscious of the discussions going on about them and who are looking for someone who can interpret what is happening at their own level and for their own guidance.

If I began with a personal testimony of my attitude to the Bible, and if I have asserted that the God whom Christians worship is the God of all truth, there should be no hesitation in following me when I assert that these are exciting and challenging times in which to be called to communicate the Christian faith. The promise that the Holy Spirit would lead men towards the fullness of truth[1] is surely being fulfilled in these days. We should welcome the current debates about the nature of God, the biblical concepts of life, the ability or lack of ability of old and young to grasp the eternal verities of the Scriptures, not because we accept without question what the progressive writers are saying, but because out of all the debates it is God's truth which will prevail.

In this spirit, then, we seek to inquire afresh into the problems of the Bible and its place within the process of Christian education. And for the purposes of our study it has been found convenient to examine these problems under three general headings. The first part deals with the Bible itself, since, unless we can resolve the questions

[1] John 14. 26.

which are invariably raised when the Bible is referred
to, our own confidence is impaired, and we cannot
teach with the conviction the subject demands. The
second part deals with the Bible as an essential factor in
Christian education, and the third with the ways in
which the Bible may be used effectively with those
whom we teach.

There may well be a temptation on the part of some
readers to examine only the last section, just as we are
sometimes tempted to see 'who done it' in a thriller,
without having to follow all the 'red-herrings' that the
writer has prepared. I hope you will resist the temptation. It cannot be said too often that the teacher's
attitude to the Bible is a prime factor. If, despite all the
insights into biblical study given to us by educational
psychologists, we are content to do what they tell us
without further question, there must be some breakdown of true Christian communication. Of all subjects,
that of Christian education is most intimately bound up
with personal relationships between teacher and pupil.
The pupil will readily sense a false attitude to the Bible
even if the teacher selects Bible passages advocated by
the expert. For this reason the question of the Bible as
the Bible is placed firmly at the beginning.

To what extent can one speak of the Bible as an
Authority? This question is not of recent origin as
might popularly be believed, nor has it emerged only
with the advent of a scientific age. The immediate
relevance of the question springs, however, from the
writings of Bultmann and Tillich, and the widespread
debate in this country on their emphasis upon de-myth-
ologising and existentialism. It has also undoubtedly
sprung from the Bishop of Woolwich with the publication of his book, *Honest to God*.[1] Their views will, of

[1] *Honest to God* by J. A. T. Robinson (S.C.M.), 1963.

course, be discussed in the appropriate place, and they are mentioned here in the Introduction to indicate that the Authority of the Bible is very much a matter of concern at the present time.

Allied to the question of Authority, but not to be confused with it, is the question of Interpretation. It would be quite wrong to assume that those who take a literal view of the Bible are the only ones who accept its authority. A cursory reading of the Fathers of the early Church is sufficient to show that verbal acceptance of the Scriptures in no way reduces the inevitability of differing interpretations. Whatever our attitude to authority as it may be found in Holy Writ, we are called upon as teachers to interpret that Holy Writ. But upon what criteria of judgment can our interpretation be based? Such criteria must include both a valid interpretation of the Word of God itself and a recognition of such interpretation as meaningful for those we teach. These are the issues to be faced in the Second Part of the book.

Finally, we have to reconcile our attitude to the Bible, and the interpretation we put upon it, with a psychological understanding of the student body, whether children or adults. If it is true that R. J. Goldman has opened our eyes to the limitations and possibilities of Bible teaching to the young,[1] much more now remains to be done in a positive way to ensure the right place of the Bible in the realms of adult education. One is aware of the ease with which child education can be criticized, but it has to be said that the twentieth century has seen a lamentable decline in serious Christian education for those who have supposedly reached

[1] See *Religious Thinking from Childhood to Adolescence* (Routledge and Kegan Paul), 1964; and *Readiness for Religion* (Routledge and Kegan Paul), 1965.

maturity. One may argue, indeed, that until adult members of the Christian Church are given the opportunity of coming to terms with the true significance of the faith they profess, and with the Bible as an essential part of their understanding of their faith, there is little hope for the future.

These, then, are the three main areas of thought we shall explore. The Bible has been placed in our hands for our own profit; it has been given so that through its pages God may reveal himself to others; it is in our hands in order that we may give it to those for whom we are responsible. It is my hope that when the exploration is ended, we may be more proud to hold it, more discerning to understand it, and more sensitive to teach it.

Part One

THE BIBLE IN OUR HANDS

1

THE BIBLE WE USE

D R. W. F. MOULTON has remarked in his book about the English Bible that 'there are probably few readers of the English Bible who are not aware that the sacred volume in their hands is but one of various translations of the Scriptures into our language'.[1] What he does not say is that there are more readers than he imagined who are aware of the variety of translations, but who still retain the idea that the real Bible, the Bible that can be trusted, is the Authorized Version.

It would be idle to pretend that the 1611 version of the Bible has not exercised a tremendous influence on the language and thought-forms of the English speaking peoples of the world; and whatever views one may hold about religion as such, the Authorized Version of the Scriptures will ever be a literary classic. Judgment upon it, for our purposes, however, must be based on the religious ideas it promotes, and the accuracy both of translation and of the selection of reliable documents upon which it is based. Translations which have appeared since 1611 may not have the same formative influence on the English language, and indeed this would seem to be improbable. But they do have the advantage of having recourse to manuscripts which were not known to exist at the time when the translators began their work to prepare the 1611 version. If a conception of the life and teaching of Christ, which forms the climax of biblical revelation, is to be as reli-

[1] *The History of the English Bible* by W. F. Moulton (Epworth).

able as possible, it is quite obvious that the Bible we use must reflect most accurately what the authors of the various books in the Bible actually recorded.

Which Bible ought we, then, to use? Some time ago I was asked to give a series of Bible lectures at a Conference, and at the first session I inquired which Bible the students had brought with them. It was discovered that a third were using the Authorized Version (though one of these was under the impression that his copy was the Revised Version); another third had copies of the *New English Bible* (New Testament);[1] the remainder had brought the Revised Version or the Revised Standard Version or one or other of the popular translations such as Moffatt and Phillips.

For the majority of students the discrepancies or differences between one version and another are so slight as to be unworthy of serious consideration, and it has to be confessed that the general impression of truth emerges whichever version is used. The scholars can, of course, point to variations in readings or in the placing of certain events which appear in different manuscripts,[2] but there have been no dramatic discoveries of earlier documents that have led to any drastic rewriting of the Bible.

The difference between one translation and another is emphasized here simply because some religious leaders and teachers do insist upon the verbal inerrancy of the Scriptures, and it has to be made abundantly clear that this approach is quite impossible when the words and phrases are different between one manuscript or version and another. Of course, if it is then agreed that 'the sense is the same' they have really shifted

---

[1] It is expected that the Old Testament section of the *New English Bible* will be published in the near future.

[2] cf. John 7. 53 to 8. 11.

their ground, and the force of their argument is lost.

There is, however, another reason for the widespread tacit assumption that the Authorized Version is the 'proper' Bible. It is, of course, the use of the word 'authorized' in the title itself. A Bible which came into existence because of Royal Command and by the exercise of Church-appointed scholars must have a special character. And this is more so when one remembers that over 250 years were to elapse before the Church decided to repeat the project. Nevertheless, other Royal Commands have been given for other versions, as for example the Injunctions drawn up under the guidance of Cranmer for the approval of Henry VIII, one of which stated, 'you shall provide ... one book of the whole Bible of the largest volume, in English, and the same set up in some convenient place within the church ... whereas parishioners may resort to the same, and read it.'[1]

Similarly, it can be pointed out that the process of translation under Church authority which was accepted for the 1611 version has been followed since. The same procedure was adopted for the production of the Revised Version of 1884, and has been followed in the recent work resulting in the publication of the *New English Bible*. It might also be added that while the authority of both State and Church is ordered differently in America, the same principle of procedure has been practised in the publication of the American Standard Version of 1901 and the Revised Standard Version of 1952. The latter version has been widely used in Britain as well as America and is held in high regard by scholars and the general public of both countries.

No one who takes his Bible seriously, therefore, and who wishes to teach it to others can afford to turn to one

[1] The reference here is to 'Matthew's' translation of 1537.

Bible and say, 'This is the Bible, and all others are defective or without authority'. He needs to examine various versions and where there is variety in translation or sequence of events note carefully the marginal references to the variant readings of the manuscripts upon which the work is being based.

One word more needs to be said about the Bible we use. Versions already referred to represent, as has been indicated, the corporate work of scholars appointed by the Church to carry out the task. In addition to such groups of translators, there have also appeared on the scene the work of certain individuals such as Moffatt, whose full translation appeared in 1926, and more recently J. B. Phillips who, having completed a series of translations of the New Testament literature, has gone on to translate into modern English the four eighth-century prophets Amos, Hosea, 'First' Isaiah and Micah. Reference should also be made to the translation of the Roman Catholic Bible (the Latin 'Vulgate') by Monsignor Ronald Knox. These works carry a freshness of translation, a significant turn of phrase, which might be expected in an individual's interpretation of what the manuscripts are seeking to say. Perhaps they should be regarded as transcriptions or paraphrases rather than translations. For an assessment or interpretation of truth as opposed to a literal translation of words they have tremendous value and appeal, and no student should be without one or other of them.

So far we have assumed that the Bible we use is, in fact, an English Bible. And behind the Authorized Version itself, which in the Church history of this country is an important turning point, there lie a number of other English versions. The inscription of the Authorized Version states 'Translated out of the original tongues and *with the former translations diligently compared*[1] and revised by His Majesty's special command A.D.1611'.

For a detailed analysis of the various English Bibles printed before 1611 the reader is invited to turn to Moulton's summary, to which reference has already been made. It is sufficient here to note that those to which the translators of the Authorized Version referred include the Geneva Bible (1560) remembered chiefly today for its translation of Genesis 3. 7, and popularly known as the 'Breeches Bible'; the 'Matthew's Bible' which was probably the joint work of two exiled scholars, John Rogers and William Tyndale; the 'Coverdale Bible' (1536) 'sett forth with the Kynges most gracious license'; and 'Tyndale's Bible'.

One may pause in recalling the place of William Tyndale in this survey of English versions of the Bible, for his life and work are illustrative of three factors which are not unimportant. The first is that the underlying concern for the production of Scriptures in the common language of the people was that they should be able to read the Bible for themselves. The theological controversies which surround the period of the Reformation should not blind us to the fact that the years leading up to that Reformation were years of increasing ignorance and superstition among the common people. The renewal of life within the Church prompted by the Reformation, therefore, included within it a desire that people should be able to take the Word of God to themselves. So we are not surprised that this desire lay at the heart of Tyndale's work. On one occasion he summed up this concern by remarking in the presence of a learned scholar, 'If God spare my life, ere many years I will cause a boy that driveth the plough shall know more of the Scriptures than thou dost.'

[1] My own italics.

The second factor worthy of recall brings us again to the interpretation we place upon the Bible in our teaching. When Tyndale's translation first appeared in England it was observed that he had used in his translation the words 'congregation' for 'church'; 'senior' for 'priest'; 'favour' for 'grace'; and 'repentance' for 'penance'. These interpretations of the text were disputed by Sir Thomas More, and for this reason in the second edition of the translation Tyndale made one correction. He revised the word 'senior' and replaced it by 'elder'. But he would not use the word 'priest'.

When one considers the significant theological distinction between 'repentance' and 'penance', its place in the controversies of the Reformation and its continuing place in Protestant versus Roman Catholic issues, one can begin to see how important it is for us to know what Bible we are using and what interpretation we are prepared to bring to it.[1] And when one enters into the present ecumenical debates on Church Orders the same problem concerning the emotive words 'priest' or 'elder', and what we imply by them, adds force to this question.

The third factor may not have the same intellectual content as the others. But it should not be forgotten. William Tyndale was not only prepared to live in exile for the sake of his conscience; he was prepared to die for his conviction that the Scriptures should become available to all. While still living abroad he was betrayed by so-called friends and was martyred in 1536. Today it is our privilege to use a Bible written in our own language, and it is freely available to us all. But that

[1] But note the *Jerusalem Bible* – officially approved by the Roman Catholic Church – has 'repent' in Matthew 3. 2, Mark 1, 15, etc. (published in 1966.)

opportunity and that freedom have not been obtained for us without a price being paid.

Scholars responsible for these versions were eager to discover the Scriptures in the original tongues of Greek and Hebrew. Before them all the versions were English translations of the Latin 'Vulgate', the most important being that of John Wyclif, the most conspicuous scholar of the fourteenth century. It was his translation which spanned the gulf between hand-copied versions of the Bible, laboriously undertaken at great cost in time, energy and concentration, and the invention of printing which in itself exercised such influence in the spreading abroad of the Word of God.

When Caedmon 'sang of the creation of the world, the origin of man, and all the history of Genesis . . . the incarnation, passion, resurrection of our Lord . . .'[1] in his own common tongue he was setting in motion a movement whose impetus would continue to the present time. It is better to face the problems of a Bible open for all to read, than to try to solve them by closing it. The light may reveal many things that disturb and give rise to anxiety. But this is better than to grope in darkness. Over the centuries men have sought to overcome the darkness by bringing to us the light of God's word in a language we can understand. It is for us now to learn to handle that word rightly.

[1] *Ecclesiastical History* by the Venerable Bede.

2

ITS FORMATION

S O FAR we have referred to the Bible as a single book standing in its own right, and by tradition regarded as authoritative for Christians on all matters affecting their faith and practice. The question now has to be asked, how did the Bible come to be the Bible? Its writings cover a period of something like a thousand years and the events described range over a far longer period than that. There are tabulated sixty-six 'books' in all, divided into Old and New Testament scriptures, not counting those in the so-called 'Apocrypha'. There also exist other religious writings, both for Hebrews and Christians, than those contained in the Bible which are available for study. On what basis was a selection made? And when made, how did the various books chosen come to be what they now are? Today we can open our Bibles, select a book of our choice, and then read chapter and verse. We are able to quote our references, and there are many advantages in so doing. But the Bible was not always like this. How, then, has the Bible come to be the Bible?

The traditional view, of course, in early Church history (but not universally accepted even then) and revived in post-Reformation years, as men sought for an infallible authority to replace an infallible Church, has been that God selected certain chosen men like Moses and the prophets, the writers of the Gospels and St. Paul, and then dictated to them what he wanted to say. There is no need to elaborate the point that such a view is an insult to man's free will and integrity, as it is to God's respect of man's free will and his own character. Nor is there need to point out, as has been done on a number of occasions, that on such a theory Moses recorded his own death,[1] God seems to have contradicted himself on a number of occasions,[2] and that, having taken the trouble to dictate his truth, God seems to have so scattered it that it is now impossible to discover what exactly was said! We must clearly look elsewhere for a proper account of the origin and formation of the Bible as we now have it. And for the purpose of clarity and simplicity it is better to look separately at the Old and New Testaments.

The Old Testament

Scholarship during the past two hundred years, and particularly that of German Bible scholars, has shown that the Old Testament is a collection of literature acquired over the centuries, and, subjected to revised forms of editorship and collation, consisting of oral sayings and stories handed down from generation to generation, to which have been added or into which have been inserted accounts of historical events, biographies, recollections or prophetic utterances, and accepted expressions of Hebrew worship.

Much of this scholarship has been detailed in its analysis and has been undertaken amid the ebb and flow of theory and speculation. Apart from the painstaking study of manuscripts there has been intensive investigation into comparisons of Hebrew mythology with that of contemporary tribes and peoples of the Middle East with a resultant awareness of the distinc-

[1] Deuteronomy 34. 7.
[2] Genesis 6. 19–22 and 7. 1–5.

tive contribution to religious thought brought to
mankind by the Hebrew people. There are some who
think that studies such as these are negative, trivial and
irrelevant. It is, however, largely because of such
investigations that the Old Testament has retained its
unique place as worthy of special consideration, and has
not just been handed over to the anthropologist as an
example of primitive thought and practice. It is because
of such investigations that new meaning is now being
attached to the unity of the Bible and an intelligent
appraisal of the theology which emerges from its pages.
If there is today a valid concept of authority derived
from the Scriptures for thinking people, that authority is
due in great measure to the work of biblical scholars
and not in spite of them.

No attempt is made here to describe this work in any
detail, and the student who needs to examine the Old
Testament in depth will have the recognized reference
books to which to turn. Our purpose is different. Yet
a brief summary of the main findings of biblical
scholarship needs to be attempted for the benefit of the
general reader.

The people of Israel were like other people in that so
many of their family and tribal customs and beliefs
were communicated in simple forms by word of mouth
to succeeding generations. They might be in the form of
riddles or rhyming sayings (remembering that 'verse' for
Semitic people is different from that in Western culture).
There were stories of heroes, legendary or real, and
'battle songs' confirming the virility and strength of
their predecessors. One ought not to be surprised that
this is so. It is true of the early histories of people everywhere.[1]

[1] Examples of biblical records of 'oral traditions', etc., may be found in
Genesis 18, 24, 28, 30; Judges 5.

Such oral traditions, including the stories of creation, the origin of man, and the development of racial tribes were only brought together in written form as 'scriptures' in the ninth century B.C. During the next one hundred years the priestly classes of the Hebrew people were at work bringing their own particular religious interpretation to bear upon the folk-lore of the people, and this meant that by 750 B.C. there were at least two strands of thought relating to the interpretation of the culture of the times. These strands can be seen in the early books of the Old Testament and help to account for the differences or discrepancies in accounts of the same events.

The most formative period in Old Testament times was undoubtedly the eighth century B.C. This was the age of the prophets whose message did so much to heighten the conception of God and to widen the horizons of men in response to him. Opposed as they were in their own time, almost without exception, the authority of their word and the significance of its truth came to be recognized, and was reflected in a third strand of thought which came to be recorded and preserved during the next century. This brings us to the year 650 B.C. during the reign of King Josiah. It was almost certainly the recordings of the prophetic messages and their implications which were 'discovered' when repairs were being carried out at the Temple, and which were to become the foundations upon which Josiah's reforming reign were to be built.[1]

Another significant turning point in the history of the Hebrew people, and one which has bearing upon the way in which the Scriptures came to be written, was the post-exilic period during which time the way of life we know as 'Judaism' came to be established. It was in

[1] 2 Kings 22.

this period that all strands were drawn together into recognized books and the shape of the Old Testament came to be determined. The reading of the Law by Ezra in 444 B.C.[1] set the seal of authority upon the first five books of the Bible, called the Pentateuch, and by 180 B.C. similar authority had been given to the later books, to complete the Old Testament.

There was, of course, other religious literature which had gained popularity, and the Jews, for the sake of order and discipline were compelled to indicate which were accepted and which were not. 'The sayings of the wise are like goads, and like nails firmly fixed are the collected sayings which are given by one Shepherd. My son, beware of anything beyond these.'[2]

The better known of such writings outside the Old Testament are collected together in the *Apocrypha*, and are in fact included in the Greek and Latin Bibles. One such book, *Ecclesiasticus* mentions in its opening paragraph those writings affirmed to be the Hebrew Scriptures and these would include all the books at present found in the Bible.

Official confirmation of a Canon of Scripture for the Jews was given at the Jewish Synod of Jamnia in A.D. 90. Josephus, the great Jewish historian described this occasion in the following words. 'We have not myriads of books disagreeing and contradicting one another, but only twenty-two . . . justly believed in'.[3] For them the Old Testament was divided into the *Pentateuch*, the *History*, and the *Prophets*. Later, however, the contents were described as *History*, *Prophecy*, and *Writings*.

---

[1] Nehemiah **8.** 1–3.
[2] Here is an obvious reference to a limited Canon of Scripture. It is found in Ecclesiastes **12.** 11, 12 and should be compared with Revelation **22.** 18.
[3] Josephus *The Works of Flavius Josephus* translated by W. Whiston.

This is an outline of the way in which the Old Testament came to be formed, without reference to the recognition of the same Scriptures by the early Christian Church. Indeed, the question has often been raised, Why do we have an Old Testament at all? Isn't the New Testament sufficient by itself? The answer is of course that Christ himself was a Jew, cradled in the Jewish religion and nurtured in their scriptures. The fulfilment of his life and teaching is to be seen within that context. 'Think not that I have come to abolish the law and the prophets; I have come not to abolish them but to fulfil them.'[1] The Gospel, in its early days, found justification for what Christ said and did in the Old Testament scriptures,[2] and every book contained in the Old Testament is quoted in some part or other of the New Testament.

The New Testament

For different reasons the beginnings of a formation of the New Testament Canon are similar to those of the Old Testament. There was a period in the early Christian Church when the communication of the Gospel, centering as it did upon the life and teaching of our Lord, was not by written word at all but by 'oral tradition'. Indeed, the first Christian writings as we now have them are not the Gospels, but the Pauline letters.

Three reasons may be adduced for an unwillingness to commit the life of Christ to a written form. In the first place, the people most able to do this were the Apostles themselves, and their commitment was to a proclamation and exposition of the Gospel. They were

[1] Matthew 5. 17.
[2] cf. Acts 2. 14–36.

not by nature literary men, nor schooled in the art of biographical exercises. They were men, called of Christ, to be his 'witnesses in Jerusalem, and in all Judaea and Samaria and to the end of the earth'.[1] The way that this was to be done was by preaching and teaching and engaging in missionary enterprise. It is fortunate that there were those who preserved what was preached and taught, for it is upon such records that the Gospels in their present form have been built.

The second reason for an unwillingness immediately to write an account of Christ's ministry was a widespread belief, shared by the Apostles themselves, that Christ would speedily return to the world and bring about the consummation of his Kingdom.[2] If this were to be so there were more important things to do than to sit down and write about him. He would soon be in their midst and the whole world would be compelled to acknowledge his power and his glory.

The third reason may be discovered in the psychological attitude of the Jewish leaders to literary works of any kind. Interest in religious biography had virtually ceased with the settlement of the Jews in the post-exilic period, and more and more attention had been directed to legal expositions and precedents for the preservation of the Law. It was only as the spread of Christianity into the Greek and Roman worlds made its own impact upon the Church leaders that a serious concern to have authentic written records of what Christ did and said was aroused.

Two kinds of written documents did, however, begin to emerge. Behind the on-going missionary enterprise of the Apostles, there were those who for their own benefit and in order to teach others, compiled

[1] Acts 1. 8. cf. Matthew 28. 18, 19.
[2] cf. Acts 1. 11; John 21. 20–23; 1 Thessalonians 1. 10.

documents which brought together 'sayings' of our Lord, sometimes as composite records in their own right,[1] and sometimes in association with a particular event in Christ's ministry.[2] These are now incorporated into the Gospels. At the same time there was need for the Apostles to keep in touch with Christian communities they had helped to establish, and so letters were written which were then passed from one church group to another as a basis for comment, discussion, and guidance. St. Paul's letters are obvious examples of this form of Christian literature.

Such limitations in the literature of the new religion could not, however, be long endured. The wider the influence of Christianity the greater the demand for authoritative accounts of what Jesus actually did and said. There were the questions of genuine seekers after truth to be met; there were the arguments of opponents, Jewish and Gentile, to be answered. So, eventually, the Gospels came to be written.

The earliest of these is Mark's Gospel, written by someone who had the opportunity to learn much at first hand from Peter. An excerpt of the writings of Papias[3] is preserved for us which states

> Mark, having become the interpreter of Peter, wrote down accurately everything that he remembered, without, however, recording in order what was either said or done by Christ. For neither did he hear the Lord, nor did he follow him; but afterwards, as I said, attended Peter, who adapted his instructions to the needs of his hearers, but had no design of giving a connected account of the oracles of Jesus.'[4]

[1] cf. Matthew 5 to 7; Luke 6. 20–46.
[2] cf. Luke 7. 36–50; 8. 19–21; 11. 45–52.
[3] Expositions of the Oracles of the Lord, quoted by Eusebius.
[4] In view of recent criticism about the quotation it is important to note that the internal evidence of Mark's Gospel entirely supports its implications.

The date of this Gospel, as with all the Gospels, is a subject for discussion, and different dates are offered by different scholars. It is generally accepted, however, that it must have been written early in the history of the Church, probably at Rome, and the date usually offered is A.D. 65-67.

The authors of the Gospels of Matthew and Luke were able to draw on Mark as part of their source material and that they did so is really beyond question. Although, as Papias says, Mark does not attempt to put into order the events of Christ's ministry, both Matthew and Luke follow the same pattern. Two-thirds of the contents of Mark are substantially used by both Matthew and Luke, and the remainder of Mark (except for some thirty verses) is used by either Matthew or Luke.

When one examines material found in Matthew and Luke which is not recorded by Mark, such material falls into two categories. In the first category so close are the parallels that it is clearly seen that the material must have come from another 'source' which they both used, and which is almost certainly an early example of documented sayings of our Lord. Scholars refer to it as 'Q' from the German word *quelle* which means source. The second category embraces the remaining parts and also has interesting possibilities.

Luke's Gospel contains material which is distinct from both Mark and Matthew and does not fit into 'Q'. It is assumed, therefore, that Luke was able to use sources which came to his knowledge during his two years' stay at Caesarea with Paul.'[1] On the other hand, the material in Matthew not belonging to Mark or Luke or 'Q' is strongly Judaistic in character, and seems to reflect the kind of way in which Christians in a fervent

[1] Acts 23. 23—24. 27.

Jewish community would need to exercise their teaching ministries. Scholars suggest that such material would be derived from sources in the Church at Jerusalem itself.

There is even more discussion on the dates of these Gospels than of Mark, but it is now generally supposed that Luke was written about A.D. 80, and that Matthew was written soon afterwards, about A.D. 85.

The first three Gospels are called 'Synoptic' because they cover the same general view, or 'synopsis' of the life of Christ.

In a survey of this kind it is not possible to analyse in turn each of the books in the New Testament; but there are three books, other than the Synoptic Gospels and the letters of St. Paul, to which some attention should be given. These are John's Gospel, the *Epistle to the Hebrews*, and *Revelation*.

We need to refer to John's Gospel because it is so different in character and purpose that it would be dangerous to infer from silence that it has to be judged as one might judge the Synoptic Gospels. The purpose of this Gospel is avowedly evangelical in character and makes no attempt to describe the life and teachings of Christ in the manner of the other three Gospels. It is written in order that 'you may believe that Jesus is the Christ, the son of God, and that believing you may have life in his name.'[1] Its construction is such that sayings of Jesus or incidents in his life are used as starting-points for the exposition of Christian truth, rather as preachers today use Bible texts for this purpose. The text of this Gospel does not always make it clear what are to be regarded as authentic words of Christ and what are comments made by the author himself.[2]

[1] John 20. 31.
[2] cf. John 3. 1-21.

Critics are far from unanimous in their explanations of the particular structure of the Gospel. Some affirm that a great deal of material belongs to Christ's own ministry in association with visits to the Temple, and that the 'events' are parables spoken by Christ before formally expounding their meaning. This was the common practice of rabbis at the time of Christ. Others believe that they are early examples of devotional addresses given by early Christian leaders prior to the celebration of Holy Communion. Certainly the Gospel would not appear to be biographical in the sense in which a historian would use that word, or even as was understood by the authors of the other Gospels. Of the spiritual insights contained in John no one can possibly be in doubt.

There is also uncertainty about the authorship of John, but opinion seems now to veer towards a recognition of the 'beloved disciple' as being responsible for it, or someone very intimately connected with him. And because of its devotional character, which rises to heights far removed from contemporary history, it is difficult to find evidence for a date of the Gospel. It may be assumed however, to be some time between the writing of the other Gospels and sometime not later than A.D. 130. If a date has to be given on probability it would be placed between A.D. 85 and A.D. 100.

Associated with the Gospel is the *Book of the Revelation*. Here, again, we are dealing with literature that is not historical or expositional or even devotional in the accepted sense of those terms. Couched in apocalyptical terms it is 'a trumpet call to faith in view of the sure triumph of the Kingdom of Christ and of God.'[1] Its references to persecution and opposition are such as to

[1] G. R. Beasley-Murray in *A Companion to the Bible* edited by T. W. Manson and H. H. Rowley (T. and T. Clark), 1963.

indicate the period of Christian persecution under Domitian (about A.D. 96). Tradition has accepted the view that the author is the same as St. John's Gospel. But this is open to grave question. Some have felt that here is an Aramaic work literally translated into Greek. Its place in the Bible can unquestionably be attributed to the mystical and majestic descriptions of the Last Days and the resounding call to Christians to remain faithful whatever befalls them. A Church which in its formative years knew the harsh realities of persecution and martyrdom could not but include it in its Canon of authoritative scriptures.

The *Epistle to the Hebrews*, although traditionally ascribed to St. Paul, is so distinctive in its language, form, and content, that all scholars are agreed that Paul is certainly not the man to have written it. All kinds of suggestions have been made, none of which has found general acceptance, and there is little point in pursuing any of the current theories of authorship. Its message is clearly directed to the Jewish community to recognize the richness and wonder of their heritage, and to take that supreme step which acknowledges the supremacy of Christ over all, whether patriarch or priest, king or 'angel of light'. It could have been written between A.D. 66 and A.D. 70 'when war clouds gathered over Palestine and appeal was made for Jews to stand together for faith and fatherland',[1] and more recently an attempt has been made to associate it with those Jews who were rejecting orthodoxy and might have been influenced by the Qumran sect, but who were looking for a final prophet to do in the latter days what Moses had done in the former.

So in the second half of the first century Christian literature, reflecting different emphases of relevance to

[1] G. R. Beasley-Murray, op. cit.

contemporary needs in the life of the Church, began to
appear. It was in the second century that the Church
Fathers began increasingly to turn to such literature to
support the exposition of Christian truths. By A.D.
175–200 Irenaeus was quoting as authoritative the
four Gospels, St. Paul's letters, 1 Peter, 1 and 2 John,
the Acts of the Apostles, and The Revelation. In the
third century Origen drew up a list of those books he
believed should be accepted by the Church, and those
which ought to be rejected.

Only with the emergence of suspect and heretical
teachings, however, which carried the convictions of
supposedly Christian prophecy, and which began to gain
a large following, was the Church led to establish a
Canon of the Scriptures relating to Christian literature.
'The best defence set up by the Church . . . was to close
the canon of scripture, and by so doing to deny any
authority to (false) prophecies.'[1] Eusebius of Caesarea
consulted the various Church bodies of his time, and in
the light of the answers he received drew up his categories of accepted books, disputed works, and spurious
'Christian' literature. The Festal Letter of Athanasius,
circulated in A.D. 367 cleared up the remaining ambigui-
ties about a Canon, and listed the books as they now
appear in our New Testament, though in a slightly different order.

Remoteness of time and freedom from the pressures
being placed upon the Church in the first four hundred
years of the Church's life might lead us to a different
selection of religious literature than that which finds
itself in the Bible today. It is worth remembering therefore, that 'the responsible teachers whose writings are
gathered together into this Canon . . . were certainly
less uncompromising than some of their followers on

[1] *A History of the Early Church* by J. W. C. Wand (Methuen), 1937.

C

the extreme wings, and they certainly did not find their interpretations mutually incompatible. Consciously or unconsciously their wise toleration made for unity in disunity'.[1]

[1] J. W. C. Wand, op. cit.

3

ITS RELIABILITY

O NE of the major problems which confronts the Christian educator is that of the reliability of the stories and events described in the pages of the Bible. This is a matter which he has to resolve for himself in his own attitude to and use of the Bible. It is also a matter of concern for those whom he teaches, since, sooner or later, whether teaching young or old, questions will inevitably be raised about the authenticity of what is found in Bible.

The relationship between the reliability and the authority of the Bible is one that will be discussed in the following chapter. Nevertheless, it is clear that for those in the nineteenth century brought up to accept the authority of the Bible without question, a shattering blow to their belief was delivered by those who seemed to undermine its reliability and accuracy. Since then, in whatever ways the world of biblical scholarship has sought to come to terms with science and history, there has been a general unease about the exact status of the Bible. Is it reliable, or isn't it?

This general unease is sharpened when we are confronted by the world of growing children who inevitably pass through a period of literal logic in their mental processes and who tend to judge all issues in simple terms of black and white, right and wrong. Either the Bible is true, or it isn't true. There can be no doubt that many boys and girls reject the Christian religion and association with the Church on the grounds that, having been brought up to accept the Bible as true, they begin to discover that it is not reliable, as they understand reliability. They have consequently abandoned all acceptance of what the Bible really stands for and have missed its true significance. It should not, however, be assumed that such a naïve logical attitude, understandable in children, is limited to children. One of the big problems in bringing home to people the relevance of the Christian faith is that of overcoming a similar barrier in the thinking process (and its attendant emotive factors) which so many of them retain from childhood.

In approaching the subject of the reliability of the Bible two extreme points of view may be adopted. On the one hand there are those who because the Bible does not reflect the thinking of a scientific age are prepared to reject the whole of the Scriptures as irrelevant and outmoded, or are prepared to defend it solely in terms of religious mythology and imagery. And the attitude of the latter may be more dangerous than that of the former. Whenever subject to cricitism their answer is invariably, 'We do not pretend that the Bible is reliable, but it does say things about God which we ought to heed'. This, it seems to me, is the logical conclusion implied by such scholars as Tillich and Bultmann, and it strikes at the heart of Christianity as a revealed historic religion.

On the other hand there are those whose built-in defences of the faith are so bound up with their attitude to the Bible that their minds automatically reject any view other than the literal biblical one. That this kind of 'bible-idolatry' does disservice to intellectual honesty, calls in question the continuing work of the Holy Spirit, and betrays a tragic misunderstanding of the purposes of God in and for the world of today, is of secondary concern compared with the retention of their own religious props. One can sympathize with simple people, bewildered by so much expertise in science and history and biblical criticism; one cannot sympathize with otherwise intelligent people who build within their minds compartments of truth and are unwilling to explore the extent to which such compartments are interconnected.

Somewhere between these extreme positions, the truth may well be found, and it is necessary at the very beginning to see that it would be wrong to select the evidence which seems to suggest the reliability of the Bible and to ignore that which does not. If statements are made about authenticity and are challenged, the right to reply can be sustained. But once that reply is given in terms of history, records, archaeological discovery, geological research, then all the evidence in such fields of study has to be borne in mind. It is, in the end, the wholeness, the unity of truth which matters. Anything less than this is unworthy of honest search for truth. The evidence we seek must be the whole truth and nothing but the truth.

It is, of course quite impossible here – or indeed anywhere else – to analyse every single story and event of the Bible and discuss its accuracy and reliability. It is much more valuable to be given ways of looking at the Bible which take account of the extent and limitation of modern knowledge and which may help to formulate a proper attitude towards the Bible. In order to help to that end, it is proposed to examine the question of reliability from three angles.

(1) Within the biblical records there is a period of well-defined history which is capable of comparison with other historical records of a contemporary nature. This period spans both Old and New Testaments, beginning with the early stories associated with Abraham and continuing up to the time of the formation and

early development of the Christian Church. To what extent can reliance be placed upon the historical events described within this period? Is the Bible myth or history, or is it both?

(2) Beyond this historical period, however, there stretch the aeons of time which go back to the origin of man and the creation of the world. To what extent can we rely upon biblical records for their description of these events? Should the stories of Genesis be taken as history or as myth? Do they belong to the mythology of primitive man, without any claim to historicity; or do they represent in dramatic form actual historical stages? It is here that the Bible most easily falls into disrepute. Is it better to admit to unreliability and to disregard what is written?

(3) But within the historical period, and assuming great significance in any appraisal of the life of Christ himself, there emerges the question of miracles. Fact or fiction? history or mythology? What interpretation can we bring to bear upon the Bible records which refer quite blatantly to the miraculous element in God's revelation to the world of men?

It is to these three aspects of biblical analysis and interpretation that we now turn.

The Historical Period

The accounts of archaeological surveys undertaken in the Middle East which may be related to Old Testament times make romantic reading. So much so that Clifford Jones has done well to remind us that 'the titles of some of the more popular books on archaeology seem to suggest that the aim of biblical archaeology is to prove the Bible is true.'[1] Certainly the surveys confirm in

[1] *Teaching the Bible Today* by C. M. Jones (S.C.M.).

amazing ways something of the veracity of biblical accounts, but, as will be shown, there is a strict limitation in the acceptance of such veracity that needs always to be observed. At the same time it would be irresponsible to regard the results of archaeological discovery as unimportant, for they serve to underline that many fanciful theories about the Old Testament which were once popular in critical circles have had to be abandoned, and a more cautious approach to its pages adopted.

For example, the digging expedition carried out under the direction of Sir Leonard Wooley in Iraq, which has led to the recognition that at some remote period of time the whole of that area had been submerged by tremendous and unusual floods, confirms a basis in fact rather than in legend for the biblical story of the Flood.[1] Such confirmation, however, still has to be limited in any conclusions drawn from it. Other parts of the world have revealed similar evidence of flooding, but there is no reason at all to suppose that the whole world was literally flooded at one and the same time. Moreover, the stories which have been built upon the accounts of the flood, and the interpretation put upon them, cannot receive the same kind of confirmation. It is not surprising that those who heard stories of a flood in former times should read into them more than can factually be sustained. If, much later, people's conception of the world was severely circumscribed, the people of Old Testament times can be forgiven for believing that the Middle East basin was in fact the whole world. To them, a tremendous deluge over that area was a deluge covering the face of the earth.

Again, one may refer to the Babylonian contract tablet which, when translated, described a farmer, Abram by name, living in the district of Ur under the

[1] Genesis 7. 11, 12.

First Dynasty, about 2200 B.C. Caiger has said of this discovery, 'Leaving details for a broader view, the biblical story of Abraham and his migration does fit in with what we know of the general situation at the beginning of the second millennium. Babylonia had already been for some centuries a centre of Semitic peoples in constant communication with their kinsmen in the west. The route from Ur of the Chaldees to Haran, Damascus, and Palestine was well known'.[1] This discovery at least indicates the strong possibility that Abraham was a particular individual and not merely a symbolic figure of a tribe or patriarchal type, and to that extent it confirms the Old Testament record; but it does not prove that all the stories written about the life of Abraham, and the interpretation of those stories, carry the same authenticity.

Other Old Testament events may be considered in a similar fashion. The recognizable signs of volcanic eruption, the nature of mineral deposits within the structure of the rocks, and geological analysis, in the region of Sodom and Gomorrah, can go a long way to explaining the destruction of those cities and the 'discovery' of a victim of that destruction seeking to flee from its danger being transformed into a 'pillar of salt'.[2] Even the story of Joseph[3] has very interesting parallels in Egyptian accounts of one who delivered Egypt in time of famine and was able to supply the needs of those less fortunate.

To those who still feel that the Bible is under pressure from sceptics whose purpose it is to show the absurdity of biblical records, systematic archaeological surveys and geological research can offer much to restore their confidence in the reliability of reference

[1] *Bible and Spade* by S. L. Caiger (Oxford University Press), 1938.
[2] Genesis 19. 24–28.
[3] Genesis 41.

to apparently extraordinary events described in its pages. But to those who still insist upon verbal inerrancy there can be given no such assurance. There are general conditions or situations which have their foundations in fact. But upon such foundations have been erected interpretations of the facts, and stories seeking to illustrate such interpretations, which may have their place in a study of the religious development of people but which must remain under suspicion when judged solely in terms of objective history.

When we turn to the New Testament, which is much more firmly established in a specific and a more narrowly defined period of history, there can be little doubt as to the veracity of its historical references, and the general authenticity of historical events described in its various books. References to such leading figures as Herod, Pontius Pilate and Felix, for example, are confirmed beyond doubt in contemporary records other than the New Testament itself. It has been said that the historicity of Jesus is better authenticated from an objective historical point of view than that of Julius Caesar.

That, from the time of the life of Christ, there emerged a new religion or sect, such as is described (in different theological terms) in the New Testament is also beyond doubt. So, for example, in the writings of Suetonius there is a reference to the expulsion of Jews from Rome, ordered by Claudius about A.D. 52 on the grounds that 'the Jews were continually making disturbances at the instigation of Chrestus'.[1] Josephus, the famous Jewish historian also refers to the Christian sect in his own account of events which took place prior to the destruction of Jerusalem in A.D. 70.[2]

[1] Almost certainly a reference to quarrels between Jewish and Christian teachers in Rome. Quoted in *Documents of the Christian Church* ed. H. Bettenson (The World's Classics), 1953.

[2] op. cit.

As with the Old Testament, so with the New, we must not, however, place upon this evidence of reliability a weight it is not capable of bearing. It is one thing to accept the historicity of Jesus; it is another to accept on similar grounds the particular interpretation of the life of Jesus that is put upon it by the New Testament writers. The one deals with the fact of Jesus; the other with a faith which he seemed able to evoke, and which may or may not be accepted by his contemporaries and those who have followed after.

The Bible may receive confirmation of its general reliability in so far as its historical context is concerned, but this by no means shows the Bible to be 'true' in any wider sense. This becomes much more a matter of intelligent understanding of the process of interpretation. And, as far as our response to Christ himself is concerned, as we ought to expect, such interpretation is determined by faith and not by the manoeuvring of facts to prove what God has intended should lie outside the realm of proof.

The Pre-History Period

Whatever comfort may be derived from archaeological surveys in so far as they confirm the reliability of biblical records in comparable historical periods, there seems to be naught for our comfort when we turn to the pre-history period.

The first matter to be disposed of is that of the conjectural dating found in the margin of some Bibles. Painstaking examination of the Old Testament records by Bishop Ussher and others produced the date 4004 B.C. as the date of creation, and some versions of the Bible actually carry this date in the margin opposite Genesis 1. 'But the chronology acceptable to scientists today requires a time-scale of the order of thousands of millions of years for the age of the solar system, and of the order of tens of thousands for the age of man on the earth.'[1]

Quite recently a petrified star-fish, embedded in rock for tens of millions of years, has been discovered 5,000 feet above sea-level in a valley of the Tadzhik Republic.[2] Roger Pilkington has described how as a boy he once explored a derelict cement quarry and found some unusual objects shaped like bones, but so heavy that he decided to send them to the British Museum for their comments. The reply came back, 'The specimens which you sent for identification are ribs, vertebrae, and a paddle bone, all of Ichthyosaurus, a large marine reptile. . . . The date would be approximately a hundred to a hundred and fifty million years ago.'[3]

Attempts have been made from time to time to reconcile the discrepancy between the two forms of dating the pre-science period. Some have sought to find in an unusual Flood an answer to the problem. Others have worked out complicated systems of counting biblical days and seasons and years in terms of eras of time. The most desperate have been those who have tried to argue that at Creation God deliberately planted fossils in rocks in order to mislead the scientists and to test the faith of man!

All such attempts, however, serve only to show the lengths to which some people will go in order to preserve an entrenched position when they feel they are being attacked. It is a strange kind of faith to which God calls us if its existence is dependent upon an attitude of

---

[1] C. M. Jones, op. cit.
[2] U.N.E.S.C.O. Features, No. 456.
[3] *In the Beginning* by R. Pilkington (Independent Press).

hostility to truth to which the Holy Spirit leads men. For God is the God of all truth, or of no truth at all. It is much better, and much more honest, to accept the view that the Old Testament was written by men for whom the world of science was quite unknown, and to concentrate upon their interpretation of creation and the origin of man than to rely on an artificial time-scale derived from a pseudo-scientific view of what they wrote.

More important than the question of the time-scale, even if allied to it, is the subject of Creation itself. The general acceptance of Newton's conception of the world led to an abandonment of a literal biblical view with its flat earth, its oval-shaped dome overhead to keep out the floods, and its pillars stretching downwards to keep the earth from drowning in the waters below,[1] though there were those who, despite the evidence, still clung to such a picture of the world. But this 'did not basically challenge the biblical conception of creation. That could still be interpreted as an event, almost precisely dateable, in which the world sprang full blown into being'.[2]

The real challenge to the biblical conception of creation was only to emerge when the careful collation of biological material undertaken by such scientists as Wallace and Darwin was made known. 'What Charles Darwin did was to assemble such a mass of data that could be convincingly explained only by a theory of evolution as to make it impossible to dismiss the idea as no more than a wild guess.'[3] Since then the theory of evolution has been subject to even closer examination among scientists themselves than by biblical scholars or theologians. No one today accepts the theory as origin-

[1] cf. Psalm 24 1, 2.
[2] *Protestant Thought and Natural Science* by J. Dillenberger (Collins).
[3] *The Church in an age of Revolution* by A. R. Vidler (Pelican), 1961.

ally propounded, but all have recognized the validity of approach to an understanding of creation as suggested by Darwin. It is clear that 'creation' did not take place in a period of six days, but from its inception has evolved over aeons of time to its present form.

One may accept or reject the various theories of the evolving of the universe and of life within that universe, of which the biblical record is one. The really important question, however, lies in the search for the cause or origin of that evolution. And here the scientists themselves are as widely in disagreement with each other as biblical interpreters. The proposition offered by the Bible that 'in the beginning God created'[1] has as much, if not more, to be said for it than any other proposition which proceeeds on the assumption that God is unnecessary to account for the existence of the universe. Here, again, the question is resolved, not by arguments of scientific fact but by faith.

This does not mean that those who interpret the story of Creation literally do not try ingeniously to reconcile the biblical accounts with modern theories of evolution. This is clearly impossible, and even if accepted does not really prove anything one way or another. The reliability of biblical records in pre-history times cannot be judged in terms of reconciling a non-scientific with a scientific view of life. If there is any reliability at all it is only to be seen in the reiterated affirmation of faith, which lies behind the early stories of Genesis, that at the heart of all things visible and invisible is the reality of God at work seeking to fulfil his purposes in and through the world of his creation.

At the same time we need to recognize that what may be scientifically or historically shown to be unreliable, ought not to be abandoned as childish and irrelevant. It

[1] Genesis I. 1.

is not without significance that the latest of the sciences, psychology and social psychology, have given clues to an understanding of the early Genesis stories which speak, not only of God at work, but also of man responding to God and his environment.

There is at a superficial level a historical unreality about the story of Adam and Eve and their 'fall' which has led people to regard the whole business as childish, crude and primitive, and not worth serious consideration. At the deeper psychological levels, however, that same story reflects insights into human nature and an understanding of relationships with which we are only now really coming to terms. In a dramatic and imaginative sense Genesis carries more truth about life than many of the so-called existentialist examples of modern literature.

If, therefore, the pre-history period as described in the Bible is assessed at a factual level, in the sense in which science and history might understand this, then it has to be accepted that such a description is untenable. If, however, that period is judged in terms of interpretation in the realms of the underlying truth beneath the facts, then it has a great deal to say that is pertinent, relevant and challenging. It is at such a level that the reliability of the Bible needs to be understood and accepted.

The Person of Jesus Christ

We have already referred to the historicity of Jesus in our survey of the biblical historical period, but it cannot be assumed that because there is little doubt about this, everything that is said about Jesus in the New Testament can be accepted without qualification. Already we have noted that St. John's Gospel cannot be regarded in the same way as the other three Gospels, and the question of the reliability of the picture of Jesus as it emerges from the New Testament was raised at the beginning of this century by Dr. Schweitzer in his book *The Quest of the Historical Jesus*.

This quest has been pursued ever since, and is, indeed, central to the controversy in contemporary theology. Scholarly research into the teaching of Jesus has to a large degree brought about a recognition of the validity and consistency of the teachings of Jesus; but there is considerable doubt about the validity of the recorded events in Christ's life.

Such doubts are not mainly concerned with the question of Jesus' existence here upon the earth, but are directed much more to the way in which he was born into the world, the way he departed from the world, and those events which are described as 'miraculous' associated with his ministry.

Serious arguments have been brought to bear upon the acceptance or rejection of a Virgin Birth, but this is recognized by most theologians as a secondary issue. Associated with the incarnation, however, are the Bible stories of shepherds and wise men,[1] which many believe to be Christian myths written into the Gospel story in order to communicate truths associated with the incarnation which could not, with the same sense of drama or imagination, be communicated in any other way. Some scholars have, therefore, insisted on a process of what is called 'de-mythologizing', in order to arrive at experiential as distinct from symbolic truth. Such a process is important and valuable in so far as it brings us to the heart of the truth to be communicated.

---

[1] An attempt is now being made to relate these stories to certain of the Dead Sea Scrolls and the Qumran Communities. See *From Judaean Caves* by A. R. C. Leaney (R.E.P.) 1961.

This same process has been directed towards the events associated with the Cross, the Resurrection and the Ascension. And it is here that serious problems arise. The writings of Bultmann, for example, seem to indicate that for him it is inappropriate, even meaningless, to ask whether the Cross and the Resurrection are to be thought of in historic terms. To him a scientific age rules out the possibility of a Resurrection and Ascension in biblical terms, and this ought to be recognized by all Christians. What is significant, in his view, is not the historical event, open to serious doubt, but rather the spiritual truth which the so-called myth seeks to present. Another contemporary theologian, Tillich, takes up the same position from a different point of view. His interest is in psychology and philosophy. For him the fundamental questions being asked by modern man need to be put alongside the answers which Christ would give to those same questions; the historical context of Christ's life is unimportant compared with his eternal, and therefore contemporary, cosmic reality.

The views of both Bultmann and Tillich have had considerable influence upon the Bishop of Woolwich who is anxious to find a Gospel which will reach man without asking him to swallow the Christian myths of a virgin birth, a miraculous resurrection, and an ascent up to the heavens. It is not possible to enter into detailed discussions on all the problems raised by theories of these kinds.[1] But underlying them all is the tacit assumption that a modern scientific age cannot on any grounds recognize the validity of miracles, and that the only way to look at Jesus is to denude the accounts of his life of all that is miraculous, and to assume that there is little or nothing about his life of historical significance. Then

[1] A useful summary for the reader is to be found in *Revolution in Religious Education* by H. F. Mathews (R.E.P.), 1966.

one can go beneath the myths built round his earthly
life to discover the eternal, and therefore contemporary,
spiritual truths relevant for modern man.

Now it is clear that if one accepts a scientific philosophy which rejects all miracles there is nothing more to
be said. But such a philosophy is based upon a view of
science as the sole criterion by which life in the totality
of its experiences must be judged. This is to take one
compartment of knowledge and to assume that all other
compartments have to be fitted into it. Such an attitude
is both arrogant and unwarranted, and is quite unaccep-
table to all good scientists. A misguided attempt to
remove from the life of Christ all supposed stumbling-
blocks in order to find favour with intellectuals is not
new, and never produces the desired results.

In a non-scientific age men found it relatively easy to
believe in supernatural powers. So many areas of life
were shrouded in mystery that the existence of gods and
demons, or God and devil, seemed to offer the only
possible explanation for the mysteries. It has become
almost axiomatic to some superficial thinkers to suppose
that as science has progressed and solved many of the
mysteries, so God, or any other spiritual force, has
become less necessary. There is little wonder that some
people are now saying that God is dead. His existence
was conjured up to solve problems which have now
been satisfactorily solved in other ways. His existence
seems no longer to be required. He was only needed to
fill in the gaps of man's lack of knowledge and the gaps
have now been closed. God is accordingly irrelevant to
life.

The time has now come for us to understand quite
clearly that 'either God is in the whole of nature, with
no gaps, or he's not there at all'.[1] For the Christian, God

[1] *Science and Christian Belief* by C. A. Coulson (Fontana) 1958.

D

is at work in all life, and his spirit operates within scientific certainty and within the soul of man. And this, interestingly enough, is really the biblical view, which does not bring in God to make up the gaps in man's knowledge, but assumes his presence in all things.[1]

Once this view is accepted, and it is an act of faith, rather than an intellectual argument which leads to its acceptance, then God is seen as the Reality at the heart of all creation; the universe, the world in which we live, the experiences of man. Miracles, if they happen at all, do not happen because God steps into the world of creation 'upsetting the works'. They happen because God is at the heart of the world and is all the time 'controlling the works'.

Everything that happens, moment by moment, is in fulfilment of God's purposes. All events are 'revelations of the total harmony of all that exists',[2] and if God for any reason rearranges that total harmony in order to reveal his purpose this is not an intervention or an interruption, even if man cannot always recognize the higher purpose or more complex harmony of that rearrangement. If, as Christians believe, the life of Jesus is unique in the revelation of God and in the history of man, one ought not to be surprised that his coming brought about rearrangements in the order of things in order that the uniqueness of that life might find proper expression.

There are, of course, many events in Christ's life popularly associated with the miraculous which could be explained by men ignorant of science and psychology in no other way. We are now able to see that if they occurred, and there is no reason to suppose that they did not, their explanation is to be found in processes of

[1] cf. Genesis 1. 1; Isaiah 45. 18–24; John 1, 1–5; Colossians, 1, 1–18.
[2] *Miracles* by C.M. Lewis (Geoffrey Bles), 1947.

healing now known and understood by modern medical science.[1] But in the end, the unique miracle of the Resurrection remains. It is not enough to suppose it to be a myth without historical roots. It is, on any reckoning, the centre of the Christian faith. If God is God, as revealed by Christ; if he is at the heart of all things; and if there is any sense in a divine purpose being worked out in a gospel offered to men, then the Resurrection is not only possible, it is inevitable.

The form of that Resurrection, the nature of Christ's appearances to his disciples after his Resurrection, the mode of his physical departure from them, may be subject to a variety of interpretations. And despite the accumulation of so much knowledge, it is still true to say that man's ability to understand and explain the precise relationship of the physical to the spiritual is only very partial. But for the Christian God is not dead; Christ himself did conquer death; and in the ever-living Christ, God continues to work out his purposes until the whole of creation finds that perfection which fulfils those purposes.

Conclusion

Can we trust the Bible when it is put into our hands and we open its pages? We can examine its historical records, we can analyse its stories of early life, we can assess its position in relation to Christ himself; and when we have done all these things the answer is still 'Yes and No'.

The critics, if they are prepared to study carefully, will find it more reliable on many counts than perhaps they have assumed. The worshippers of its pages, on

[1] cf. *Psychology, Religion and Healing* by L. Weatherhead (Hodder and Stoughton), 1951.

the contrary, will find much that may disturb. But the honest inquirer, with faith in his heart, will find that which challenges and illumines and confirms his faith. It is not a text-book of science; it is not objective history recording events. It is an amazing account of a people to whom God revealed himself, and who therefore interpreted all life in terms of him. Without being blind to the lessons of science and history, we can read with increasing respect what it tells us of God, and, through that, what it tells us of ourselves in relation to him and our fellow-men. In this sense the Bible is not only reliable; it becomes, properly understood, the essential authority in all matters of faith.

4

ITS AUTHORITY

MANY years ago Professor Peake said, 'It is one of the infirmities of human nature to desire an infallible authority. And the authority is sought now in Scripture, now in the Church, now in inward personal illumination.'[1] Certainly the history of the Christian Church reflects the shifts of emphasis from one to another in the unceasing quest for an authority that will form a sound basis for the Christian faith. And while it may be recognized objectively that if there is any authority at all for the Christian faith it must be seen as an amalgam of church tradition, biblical record and private conscience, yet for individuals or groups of Christians the weight of authority tends to rest more firmly on one of the three, and a nicely preserved balance of all three seems difficult to achieve.

There are those for whom the search for authority appears to be a sign of weakness, and indeed at the present time one theological school of thought seems to be suggesting that man will never reach true maturity until he discards altogether the authority of a paternalistic God. These, however, are only substituting one form of private judgment or conscience as the sole criterion of authority for another form. There are also those who use an accepted authority as a refuge from the challenges of life which seem to attack the strongholds of their faith. It has always seemed strange to me that

[1] *The Bible; its origin, its significance, and its abiding worth* by A. S. Peake (Hodder & Stoughton).

even intellectual Christians, representing one tradition of the Church, will refuse to assert what they believe about moral and social problems of their time until the authority of the Church has been sought to indicate what they ought to believe about such matters. It is equally strange that many either refuse to believe, or deliberately ignore, certain scientific truths because they can find no warrant for them in the literal words of the Scriptures.

A proper understanding of the Bible may lead to an awareness of its authority for professing Christians, but it can neither be an absolute, infallible authority, nor can it be the sole authority. To claim such unquestioning authority is to substitute an interpretation of written words, themselves only translations of original words, the precise exactitude of which is in doubt, for a life of faith. One may accept the testimony of Scripture itself and firmly believe that it is inspired by God, and 'profitable for teaching',[1] but to go beyond this is to go beyond what the Bible itself says.

Historically, the Bible as the unquestioned authority for Christian believers has been accepted from the time of the Reformation which led to the rejection of the authority of the Church to the time of critical examination of the Bible records and the advent of the scientific age. It should not be imagined, however, that a tacit and uncritical acceptance of the authority of the Bible has led to unanimity of thought about the nature of Christianity, and that if only people stopped criticizing it, all would be well. One can agree that nothing is more likely to disrupt the fellowship of Christians or bring the Church into greater disrepute than a blind acceptance of the Bible as an authority that must remain above controversy. There may be bitterness expressed between

[1] 2 Timothy 3. 16.

the fundamentalists and those who do not accept a fundamentalist position. But this is often nothing compared with the bitterness which can exist among fundamentalists themselves.

One may quote, for example, the English Separatists who presented to the world 'a babel of dissenting schisms and mutual excommunication. One of the oddest aberrations was the act of at least two English Anabaptists in baptizing themselves, on the ground that there was no pure church to receive them.'[1] The present position of fundamentalist Protestantism in America is sufficient to show that an uncritical acceptance of the biblical record produces the opposite of what Christ clearly desires of his followers. There is obviously something wrong with an 'authority' which makes every individual both judge and jury of interpretation and which brings Christ's Church into open ridicule and contempt.[2]

Chadwick[3] has also reminded us of the abortive attempts in the fifteenth century to use the Scriptures to prove that the Scarlet Woman[4] of the Revelation was really to be identified with the Pope of Rome. Sects emerge today who so interpret the Scriptures as accounts in detail of the whole history of man that they dare even to date the end of the world. Fortunately, or unfortunately, not one has so far proved to be right!

More important for our purpose, however, is the recognition that a saint of God like John Wesley, whose influence in evangelism and social reformation has been world-wide, was prepared to take account of the scholarship of his day in assessing the Scriptures and for this reason wrote his own Notes on the New

---

[1] *The Reformation* by O. Chadwick (Pelican), 1964.
[2] cf. 2 Peter 1. 20—2. 3.   [3] op. cit.
[4] Revelation 17. 4.

Testament. He also took upon himself the responsibility of removing certain psalms from his hymn-book because he regarded them as unsuitable for use in public worship. He certainly regarded the Bible as authoritative, but he had too much sense to claim for it an authority that could not be sustained, and by his actions showed that he did not regard it as infallible.

But most important of all one should recall the attitude of Christ himself to the Scriptures. Most New Testament scholars agree that, in matters of temporal knowledge, Jesus was limited to knowledge shared by his contemporaries. In becoming man, he accepted the conditions of men as they existed at the time of his life upon earth, and such superior knowledge as he may have possessed lay only in the realms of spiritual insight which stemmed from his unique relationship with God. Jesus, however, despite his limitation of knowledge, but because of his supreme spiritual wisdom, was resolute in refusing to accept the Scriptures as an infallible authority, to be accepted without question. To the Pharisees, who were only too ready to rest their teaching upon that kind of authority, he said 'You study the Scriptures diligently, supposing that in having them you have eternal life; yet, although their testimony points to me, you refuse to come to me for that life'.[1]

Intelligent readers may well think that the days have long passed when one needed to consider seriously the authority of the Bible from the standpoint of verbal accuracy, 'a dictation' from God himself, as infallible for all Christians. It is my experience, however, that many who teach the faith, in day-schools and Sunday Schools, cling to such a view, and feel that their confidence is undermined when discussions of this kind are brought out into the open.

[1] John 5. 39.

The evidence that this is so may be found in the views of children themselves, the majority of whom seem to grow up with a firmly fixed view that somehow or other the Bible is God's Book and that he therefore wrote it himself, or dictated it to men who then wrote down what he said. Goldman quotes the six-year-old who, when asked how the Bible came to be written, answered in the words, 'God did it, on his typewriter'.[1] This is only one kind of response. Many similar ones could be quoted by other teachers who work regularly with children or boys and girls. In some way, the idea, however vague, is implanted that, because the Bible is a special book, God did dictate it.

It is wearisome to go over the oft-covered ground of apparent contradictions and discrepancies in Bible records. But the case for verbal inspiration needs to be proved wrong once and for all if a healthy approach to the Bible is to be obtained and a legitimate case for its authority is to be established. Let us, therefore, look at the Scripture itself. A text which has already been quoted now deserves more detailed examination.

In 2 Timothy 3. 16, 17 we find the reference to the inspiration of the Scriptures. The Authorized Version states, 'All scripture is given by inspiration of God'. The statement is clear and unequivocal. In the Revised Version, however, the same text is translated 'Every scripture inspired of God is profitable'. Here is a qualification which suggests that if the Scripture is inspired, then it is profitable. Other versions have similar kinds of translations, some favouring the one interpretation, and others favouring the other. The change is slight, and yet quite significant. As far as the manuscripts themselves are concerned there are similar differences,

[1] *Religious Thinking from Childhood to Adolescence* by R. J. Goldman (Routledge and Kegan Paul).

or the operative verb is missing altogether. It is inconceivable if God literally dictated the Bible to men that he should leave such a text, the very text which deals with the inspiration of the Scriptures, open to doubt, or capable of two views so different in meaning one from the other. To accept such an idea is ludicrous and absurd. It is the last refuge of people more concerned to protect themselves in their attitude to the Bible than to consider the character of the God they profess to worship.

In any case, as W. Neil has properly pointed out, 'a uniqueness that derives from a refusal to submit the subject to critical examination and comparison is easily won and of little value. It is quite another matter when the same conclusion is reached as a result of the most searching criticism and a careful sifting of the evidence'.[1] The authority of the Bible cannot be upheld on the grounds that it is God-given and beyond criticism. Its authority is, in fact, derived from a true understanding of its nature, arrived at after a process of criticism and because of the results of that criticism. The paradox of our time is that the authority of the Bible is now again a matter of serious consideration because it has passed through the fires of scrutiny, analysis, and scholarly examination.

The Bible does not pretend to be a scientific statement on the nature of creation, nor does it claim to be an objective account of historic events. It does, however, claim to be a book which reveals the nature and purpose of God in relation to the world of his creation. Upon this, and upon this only, can it be fairly judged.

The Old Testament may reveal a peope who accepted many of the myths and legends common to their contemporaries, but it also reveals a people whose

[1] *The Rediscovery of the Bible* by W. Neil (Hodder & Stoughton) 1958.

interpretations of those myths and legends set them apart as distinctive and unique. A comparison of the ways in which such stories have been recorded make it quite clear that the Hebrews possessed a gift of spiritual insight and discernment which illuminated the whole idea of the nature and purpose of God, not found among any of the other races of the world. From this perspective one is amazed, not by the similarity of biblical stories to others of the Babylonian people, but by the difference in description and interpretation of such stories. 'The religion of the Old Testament makes a radical break with all the other religions of the world.'[1]

Thirty years ago it was fashionable to write off the stories of creation, the origin and fall of man, as crude and primitive. Today we can recognize spiritual and psychological insights which stand comparison with a modern understanding of man and his place in the universe. To discard these stories of Genesis is to discard the painting of a master because the frame is old-fashioned.

Moreover, it needs to be recognized that the penetration of spiritual insight of the Old Testament writers is not derived from abstract thought and intellectual discussion. It is derived from the life-situations and living experiences of those described in the pages of the Old Testament. There is no attempt to prove the existence of God by argument or logical proposition. God is assumed throughout to be the ground of all being, at the heart of all that happens. Nor is there any attempt to edit the Scriptures so that the best of what is believed about both God and man is preserved and other aspects removed. The insights only came after much misunderstanding and stumbling towards the truth. The Bible is a book which deals with

[1] W. Neil, op. cit.

life, and life itself is not fitted into artificial patterns, with all the imperfections carefully removed.

Those features of the Old Testament which have sometimes been regarded as a weakness, are in fact part of its strength. Of course there are anthropomorphic conceptions of God; of course the heroes are not always saints, but also sinners. These elements confirm the view of God revealing himself within the historical content of a developing people, and of man, human and fallible, not always responding to the highest within him, but sometimes repenting when awareness is brought to him of his sin. To take away such accounts in the biblical records is to rob them of their greatest asset, which is the realization that God's truth emerges out of life itself and is not brought into man's thinking in order to account for life. Of this fact, the Old Testament is a supreme and unique record.

Here, perhaps, one needs to insert an observation that will be developed in the last part this book. One does not assume that because the Bible, and particularly the Old Testament, must be seen in its entirety, it is therefore possible to teach any part of it to anybody, whatever his age, simply because it is in the Bible. Selections of teaching and devotional material have to be made. At the same time, the need for selecting material for specific purposes does not mean that the Bible, or the Old Testament, as a whole can be disregarded, nor that it is assumed to be on the same level of inspiration as any other literature from which selection might be made.

The need to see the Bible as a whole stems not only from an awareness of revelation through history, through life situations embedded in history, but also from the realization of a unity of truth which emerges from a study of its pages. Not all the Bible reaches the heights of Psalm 23 or Isaiah 52–53. Not all prophets possess the insight of Amos or Hosea. But out of the experiences of individuals and communities there is forged a unity of purpose in the desire to interpret all life from the standpoint of God and his purposes for mankind. Professor Peake has expressed this admirably when he says, 'The point on which I should desire to lay stress is the collective witness given by experts in the deep things of God. So long as we are pre-occupied with individuals we are exposed to the serious peril of subjectivity, but when we turn from the single expert to the experts in a body we find the eccentricities of individuals may be controlled by the testimony of the whole number.'[1] It is the very multiplicity of writers and documents, with their varying degrees of wisdom and understanding, yet in all their ways pointing in the one direction which gives the Bible its strength and indicates where its unity is to be found.

All of this finds its climax, its unique expression, in Christ himself. In him the study of the Scriptures, both Old and New Testaments, becomes one. For a full appreciation of God's revelation in Christ, one needs to come to terms with the whole content of Old Testament teaching. 'Think not that I have come to abolish the law and the prophets. I have come not to abolish them but to fulfil them,'[2] said Jesus. The Old Testament must be seen 'as the essential preparation for the coming of Christ, and our own inheritance as members of the Christian Church, which is the New Israel.'[3]

In so far as Christ gathers into himself the supreme revelation of God and his purposes for the world of his creation, to that extent he gathers unto his own person

[1] A. S. Peake, op. cit.
[2] Matthew. 5. 17. (R.S.V.).
[3] W. Neil, op. cit.

the corporateness of truth to be found in the Scriptures themselves. He is the key to the unity of the Bible, a unity which is reflected in 'dramatic' or living terms rather than in abstract philosophical terms. Only as this is possible can one speak of a Bible theology – a coherent body of teaching – established in a serious assessment of the Scriptures, and therefore worthy of serious study. And it is here that the authority of the Bible may be said to hinge upon the authority of the Church and upon the conscience of man. The corporate life of Christians throughout the ages, gathered together in the on-going worship and witness of the Church, confirms and re-interprets biblical theology, and at the same time speaks with relevance, or convicting power, to the individual.

It is here, too, that one meets one of the fundamental issues of debate at the present time. Some are prepared to abandon the biblical, theological concepts of God long established, in an attempt to recast concepts more in accordance with the contemporary age. To do this they will abandon the imagery of biblical language; they will de-mythologize to the point of expurgating from the Bible all that does not accord with their idea of scientific truth; they will refashion notions of God to fit into their accepted pattern of thought.

It is one thing to reinterpret biblical truths into terms intelligible to a modern age; it is quite another to abandon them for others that seem more acceptable. If ever there was danger in making God after man's own image it is at the present time, and this is because the anchorage of biblical revelation has been removed. The more deeply one studies the Bible, the more one moves beyond the external framework to the truth which abides, and which belongs to life in all its mani-fold relationships between God and man, and man and man. The fundamentalist or literalist may be obsessed with the frame, and insist that the framework is more important than the truth within. But those who would dispense with the Bible are so concerned to establish their own framework that the truth they proclaim has to fit into their frame. Both are misguided. In the end, as the whole history of the Church affirms, it is the Bible which challenges man; it is not man who can judge the Bible. His critical faculties will be brought to bear upon it, his intelligence will be stretched to come to terms with it. But properly understood, it is he who will stand in awe of the truth which emerges.[1]

Part of the biblical revelation of God is the awareness of created man as a free agent. The authority of the Scriptures may stand in its own right as a supreme and unique record of God's reality and purpose, but man retains the right to accept or reject the record and the reality of God behind the record. It is important to note, therefore, that there is within the Bible that which confirms or denies man's own experiences with God. Because the Bible is not an abstract text-book, but a book dealing with life, embedded in history, it echoes the experiences of man, in all sorts of conditions, and reflects what God seeks to offer through such experiences in the fulfilment of his purpose. 'The measure of any authority which the Bible may possess lies in its direct religious value, open to discovery in experience . . . and in turn related to the experience out of which the Scriptures came.'[2]

This aspect of biblical authority has already been discussed in two previous publications.[3] It needs to be

---

[1] cf. H. F. Mathews, op. cit. (chapter 2).
[2] *The Authority of the Bible* by C. H. Dodd (Nisbet).
[3] See my *Teaching the Christian Faith Today*, chapter 9; and *The Experiential Approach to Christian Education*, chapter 3.

added, however, that the notion of the Bible as an authoritative confirmation of Christian experience is something to which the Church has found it necessary, again and again, to return. The *Didache*,[1] bringing light to the practice of the Church in the latter part of the first century and the second century, indicates the emphasis placed upon the required study of the Old Testament and the teaching of the Apostles in all Instruction in the Faith. By the third century it was common for those wishing to enter the Church to receive at least three years' instruction, much of which was related to an exposition of the Scriptures for an understanding of Christian doctrine and morals.[2] The beginning of educational institutions, as for instance by Charlemagne in the eighth century or by eighteenth-century Christian denominations in Great Britian, was promoted for the study of the Scriptures. There is overwhelming evidence on every hand that whatever sophistication in educational theory may exist, the training of both young and old in the meaning of Christianity remains incomplete without seeking to confirm its truth in the biblical records.

It is not possible to accept the Bible as an infallible authority, and it is a confession of weakness and a lack of the kind of faith God demands of us, to want to do so. It is unreasonable to search the Scriptures for those aspects of truth which he seeks to reveal in other ways and at other times. To want to do so is a denial of the continuous unfolding of God's truth by the work of his Holy Spirit. Such limitations in an approach to the Bible, however, in no way diminish the authority with which it can speak of those ultimate values and truth

---

[1] i.e. *The Teaching of the Twelve Apostles*. (Discovered in Constantinople, 1875.)

[2] cf. *The Egyptian Church Order*.

which lie beyond the realms of knowledge and point to the realms of faith.

As men are prepared to search for that word of God which lies beneath the words on the page, as men penetrate to the heart of Bible truth, so its authority is revealed. It confirms the experience of man in his quest for God and God's outreaching love for him; it abides, from age to age, as a record of God's revelation of that love; it points always to that which, whatever its historical content, possesses contemporary significance. And if these treasures are in earthen vessels it is because God himself desires that men should never be satisfied with the vessels themselves, but only with what they contain.

PART TWO

ITS USE IN CHRISTIAN EDUCATION

5

HISTORICAL SURVEY

THE Bible is not only placed into our hands for our own enlightenment and as a reliable authority to which we can turn for the confirmation or development of recognized Christian interpretations of life; it has also been placed into our hands for the guidance of others. Reference was made to this in the previous chapter, and despite the present tendency to depreciate the study of history as a valid means of properly understanding the present, it is worthwhile giving some attention to this historical survey. Those who are only too ready to dispense with the Bible in the communication of the Christian religion do well to see what they are doing in the light of long centuries of Christian practice in this matter.

Church history is naturally concerned with those outstanding and significant events which have helped to shape the life of the Church, and it is not always realized that while those events were taking place the normal process of educating into the faith was still being continued. From time to time the Church has been caught up in dialogue and discussion, in persecution and upheaval; yet there has been no suspension of Christian education until the debates have been finished, or the opposition overcome.

At the same time the process of education could not fail to be influenced by these events. Indeed they would not have made an abiding impression upon the Church had they not found their way into its educational programme. And these factors have to be borne in mind when one attempts to assess the place and interpretation of the Scriptures in the educational life of the Church.

In this regard the Apostolic Age is of particular significance. Whenever the Church seeks to reassess its position it invariably does so by reference to that particular age. We speak of the need to return to fundamentals, or the need for revival, or the need for renewal, and this usually involves an attempt to re-discover what the Church was like and what it sought to do in those times which come most nearly to the times of Christ himself. This is not ingenuously to assume that the early Church was ideal. Any study of St. Paul's letters will show the folly of such an assumption. Rather is it to indicate a belief that the beginnings of the Church's life established those principles upon which it should properly be built. All that has followed has been a natural development or application of those principles.

To know, therefore, the place of the Scriptures in the Church's teaching ministry is to discern something of what God himself intends. We cannot return to the Apostolic Age and reproduce in our own time the same conditions; but we can learn something of the principles which governed the practice of the Church at that time and learn from them.

The Apostolic Age was, of course, preoccupied with momentous issues. The universal application of a faith which broke down all barriers of religious sectarianism, racial distinctions, age and sex divisions; the formulation of a theology that could be more than a match for the legalism of the Hebrews, the philosophy of the Greeks, or the pagan worship of the Romans; the promotion of a way of life that led to freedom without irresponsibility and loyalty to authority without servitude; all these needed to be done, even while the Church was committed to a continuing and expanding ministry of preaching and teaching. New converts, Jews and Gentiles, needed to be grounded in the lessons which alone could give stability and bring understanding to the newly-found faith. In what sense, under these conditions, can it be said that the Scriptures had their part in such teaching programmes?

In the early days of the Church the majority of Christians were those won over from the Jewish religion. And for Jews there already existed a form of universal educational system. Compulsory education was the rule for all over six years of age. Schools, of one kind or another, were established in every town. The sessions might be in the open-air or in synagogues and there were also centres called 'school-houses'.[1] And because of the unique relationship of religion and race there was a carefully worked out scheme of religious education ritually observed in all Jewish homes. 'We have heard with our ears, O God, our fathers have told us what deeds thou didst perform in their days, in the days of old.'[2] Up to the age of ten teaching was based entirely upon the Old Testament. Between ten and fifteen years of age there was instruction in the Traditional Law and for those able and willing to continue beyond the age of fifteen there were opportunities for higher studies which included discussion on theological issues.

Thus the Jewish converts were quite ready to accept the necessity for education promoted by the Church and to accept obligations to establish Christian ritual in their own home life. But at first the early Christians

[1] *Everyday Life in New Testament Times* by A. C. Bouquet (Batsford), 1953.
[2] Psalm **44.** 1.

still continued their association with synagogue and temple.[1] Only with the persecution of the Christians by the Jews and the eventual destruction of Jerusalem in A.D. 70, which led to the dispersion of the Jews, was their association really severed.

By then, however, the tradition had been established. Church teaching, centred upon the Scriptures, Christian practices, centred upon the home; these were the two pillars upon which education was to be founded. Moreover, because Jesus himself was regarded as the fulfilment of Old Testament prophecy, there was no hesitation on the part of the Church about continuing to base much of its teaching on the Old Testament, if only to prove that Christ did in fact fulfil the hopes expressed in those Scriptures.[2] The new dimension, however, was to be seen in Christ himself. The law of the Old Testament was rigid and limited, and Christ himself was the key to the fulfilment of that law which released men from its rigidity and limitations.[3]

This emphasis on the teaching function of the Church is not introduced simply because we are dealing with the subject of Christian education. It is dangerously easy to dramatize the expanding missionary zeal of the early Church and the proclamation of the gospel, but it gives an unbalanced picture of the life of the early Church. St. Paul did not go racing around from place to place; there were periods when he saw the necessity for patient instruction and when he remained with one community until he was sure that the proper grounding in the faith had taken place.[4]

A study of the New Testament shows that the

---

[1] cf. Acts 2. 46; 3. 1; 5. 12; 13. 14, etc.
[2] cf. Acts 2. 14–36; 3. 12–26; 7. 2–53.
[3] cf. Acts 15. 1–22.
[4] cf. Acts 11. 26; 18. 11; Coloss. 1. 28; 1 Timothy.

three main elements in instruction were as follows:

(i) To show beyond any doubt that Christ, in his life and teaching, fulfilled the Old Testament prophecies.

(ii) To underline those aspects of Christian theology which went beyond the Old Testament and which found their origin in the life and teaching of Christ himself as recalled by the Apostles.

(iii) To apply these two bases of teaching to the personal, social, moral and spiritual life of inquirers and converts. All these were then translated into terms of Christian worship and fellowship to be practised as Christians came together and when they met in each other's homes.[1]

It was this form of teaching which later helped the Church to ride out the storms of private interpretation, of false and fanatical enthusiasms, and of heresy. For, as we have already seen, the New Testament came into being as a recognized expression of Apostolic teaching and this, with the Old Testament, established a Bible-centred source of Christian truth against which all teaching might be judged. 'What is called the Apostles' Instruction proves the antiquity of the belief in the Christian Church, that its doctrine must be traced back to the Twelve, who were the immediate companions of the Saviour. The idea first appears in the later epistles of St. Paul.[2] It was believed that the whole corpus of the teaching of the Church was derived from that of the Apostles during their sojourn at Jerusalem.'[3] If this is so, it gives strength to the idea that the Old Testament and Apostles' Teaching (to be incorporated later into a

[1] cf. Acts 2. 5–42.
[2] Ephesians 2. 20
[3] *Acts of the Apostles*, Moffat Commentary, F. J. Foakes-Jackson (Hodder and Stoughton), 1931.

Canon of New Testament Scriptures) were in fact the basis of Christian instruction.

The importance of the teaching ministry of the early Church may be observed in that the function of teaching was at first limited to the Apostles themselves,[1] and that when the burdens of administration seemed to limit the opportunities for preaching and teaching others assumed the administrative responsibilities so that their prime functions could continue without hindrance.[2] Only as the Church extended its influence beyond the range of Jerusalem and its environs, were other arrangements made to ensure a continuing teaching ministry of the highest order.

'Within our community God has appointed, in the first place apostles, in the second place prophets, thirdly teachers,'[3] wrote Paul. Whether this be interpreted as a strict definition of priorities in church order or not, it is clear that the teaching ministry was held in high esteem and felt to be essential for the true life of the Church. It is a sad commentary on so much of modern church organization that the teaching of the faith seems to be of less importance than the stewardship and organization of the Church. The Church in its early life had very different ideas about priorities!

An outstanding discovery in the nineteenth century was that of a document called the *Teaching of the Twelve Apostles* or the *Didache*, to which reference has already been made, and which gives evidence of church life towards the end of the first century and into the second. This document underlines what has been already said. Authority to preach and teach was given in the first instance only to the Apostles themselves. It then states

[1] cf. Acts 5. 42.
[2] Acts 6. 2-6.
[3] 1 Corinthians 12. 28.

that others, given the same authority, received that authority from the Apostles themselves. Out of such arrangements emerged the order of bishops, responsible for the Church's mission in the large towns and cities, and then to the environs of such populated areas. The bishops, like their predecessors, were expected to concentrate on preaching and teaching, and only when this was physically impossible were they empowered to call others to share in these pastoral, evangelical and educative offices.

The precise nature of the teaching itself was summarized in the *Didache* under five headings. These were, Instructions in the Faith; The Life of Asceticism; The Life of Worship; The Ministry; and Preparation for the Coming of the Lord. Sections on the Faith and the Coming of the Lord were based almost entirely upon the Scriptures themselves, the Old Testament and the Apostles' Teaching.

No one can doubt the pre-eminence given to the study of the Bible, and if any still have reservations it is enough to quote Eusebius who in referring to the persecution of the Christians under Diocletian (A.D. 303) stated, 'Imperial edicts were published everywhere ordering that the churches be razed to the ground, *that the Scriptures be destroyed by fire.*'[1]

The emphasis upon the Scriptures was not, however, maintained without creating some difficulties. We have already seen that it became necessary to define what were authoritative Scriptures by the establishing of a New Testament Canon to be put alongside the Old Testament Canon. It also became necessary for the Church itself to approve the interpretations placed upon the Scriptures by those appointed to teach. Vincent of Lerins in 434 found it necessary to write 'Since the canon

[1] My own italics.

of Scripture is complete, and is in itself abundantly sufficient, what need is there to join to it the interpretation of the Church? The answer is that because of the very depth of Scripture all men do not place one identical interpretation upon it. The statements of the same writer are explained by different men in different ways, so much so that it seems almost possible to extract from it as many opinions as there are men. ... Therefore, because of the intricacies of error, which is so multiform, there is a great need for the laying down of a rule for the exposition of Prophets and Apostles in accordance with the standard of the interpretation of the Church Catholic.'[1]

One can see the danger of a rigidly contrived interpretation authorized by the Church, which might upset the balance of an interrelation of authority between Church and Scripture. It would be an exaggeration to affirm that today there are as many different interpretations as there are teachers; nevertheless the confusion created in the minds of both young and old, when confronted by so many diverse interpretations, leads one to recognize that there must, in our day and age, be some redressing of the balance between Church and Scripture on this matter.

We have not here the time or space to trace the place of education in the Church's life in its later years of prosperity under Roman beneficence and then through the years of the decline of the Roman Empire. It is sufficient to say that in all those years, whatever was lost in spiritual integrity, in opportunities for public worship and in actual power, the precious gift of Scripture itself was preserved, and sacrificial care and painstaking labour on the part of hundreds of unknown Christian scholars and clerks, helped to keep alive

[1] 'Commonitorium', quoted in *Documents of the Christian Church*.

the records of Scripture for succeeding generations. It was this which helped to lay the foundations of the Renaissance. It was this same factor which in turn led more and more to see that Reformation of the Church was a dire necessity. Attempts in terms of 'administrative, legal, or moral reformation'[1] were abortive. It was only when a renewal of study of the Bible itself, and an exposition of Bible truth, broke through the entangled discussions of Church organization and order, that the flames of the growing reforming spirit were fanned into a blaze.

Since then, the Protestant churches and, particularly through the influence of Jesuits, the Roman Catholic Church too, have afforded the Scriptures a central place in their teaching ministries. During the past two hundred years tremendous strides have been taken in the whole field of education. Universities and colleges, secondary and primary schools, experiments in adult education, all these have been developed and are yearly being extended. Almost without exception, however, the beginnings have been found in a concern to preserve Christian culture, to widen the frontiers of Christian understanding, to make the Bible truly an open book for all.

Today the emphasis upon scientific education and the rapid growth of technical education to meet the needs of a technological society brings the classical and historical foundations of education under pressure. Primary and secondary schools are considering the introduction of a study of the humanities to replace Religious Instruction, and those who would retain the teaching of religion are unsure about the place of the Bible in that instruction. It is to this subject that we shall turn in the last section of this book. One can only say

[1] O. Chadwick, op. cit.

here that to discard two thousand years of experience, and to assume that the Bible now has no place in a sound educative process ought not to be accepted without soberly weighing up the consequences.

I must affirm my own conviction that whatever we may still have to learn about the proper use of the Bible in Christian education, to abandon it or reduce it to a 'source material' on equal terms with all other available material, would be a disastrous step to take. The need of our time is not to by-pass the Bible, but, with intelligent understanding, to restore it to a central place in the lives of those whom we seek to introduce to the Christian religion.

6

A TEXT-BOOK FOR CHRISTIANITY

THE recurring emphasis on the Bible as the mainspring of Christian education in the history of the Church, together with a recognition of its place as an objective (even if not infallible) authority in the assessment of Christian belief, would seem to reinforce the view that the Bible should retain a central position in any syllabus of Christian education. The question has, therefore, to be honestly faced, 'Why are difficulties now being put in the way of those who wish to teach the Bible?' There are those who are ready to say that, if the Bible has served so well in the past, what are the factors which give rise to a new appraisal? Why is it necessary to modify the traditional position? Is the Bible the text-book of Christianity, or isn't it?

Some of the difficulties would be removed if more people were skilled in the presentation of Bible material and were released from the imprisonment of an extreme conservative if not literalist view of the Scriptures. There is ample evidence that children are bored by the superficial repetition of Bible stories, and are confused by crude attempts to discredit the findings of science or of modern biblical scholarship. But there is little to be served by hiding behind misinformed and poor forms of teaching. The problems associated with teaching the Scriptures go deeper than that.

In the first place, it needs to be recognized that, for the first time in our history, we are dealing with a situation in which education to a secondary level, and increasingly to higher levels than that, is universal. Intellectual problems which arise in connection with biblical study are no longer confined to an intelligent minority. The days when the vast majority permissively accepted biblical authority, even when not responding to it in practice, have now gone. One should not be surprised that the controversies of the nineteenth century, scarcely understood, or ignored, by the ordinary people, should now be the concern of the masses. The teacher can no longer assume that his pupils are in the frame of mind to accept Bible teaching because it is based upon an 'authoritative' book. On the contrary, he has to recognize at the outset that, as the pupils reach the age when they begin to think for themselves, they will have all sorts of questions to ask about the Bible. Indeed, it may well be that a deliberate emphasis upon the Scriptures as 'God's Word', to be accepted without question and offered to young children, may lead to a violent reaction of rejection at a later stage.

Secondly, it is becoming increasingly evident that however carefully the Bible may be taught in terms of its authority and reliability, the contents of the Bible are in themselves difficult for children and boys and girls to understand. The very fact that it is easy to refer to the Scriptures, both Old Testament and New Testament, as a single book, adds to those difficulties. We may be able to discern the distinction and defend the close association of the two Testaments, but for many there is hopeless confusion. The public comments of people in privileged positions are not always free from the assumption that an Old Testament text carries the full weight of Christian judgment, even when it is abundantly clear that such a text is contrary to real

Christian belief. 'An eye for an eye, a tooth for a tooth'[1] is a phrase too commonly heard on the lips of Army Generals and City Magistrates for comfort. Younger people are frequently led into a maze of insecurity and doubt, and become bewildered by differing views of God and his will for men.

This inability to come to terms with the true character of God from the various records of Scripture is underlined in an age in which there are decreasing numbers of Christian homes and families. Children gain more from the indirect teaching and example of their parents than from any lessons taught in church and school. The very closeness of relationship with Christian parents enables the right interpretations to be made and doubts to be put in proper perspective. If this natural process of Christian education is removed, the children are often left with their confusions, and have no supporting environment or spiritual security to aid them.

Thirdly, and at a deeper level, so much of the Bible can only be appreciated when the literal words of the text are translated into terms of spiritual symbolism or insight. Many stories which, out of a false sense of reverence, are told with solemnity as being 'gospel truth' ought to be interpreted as exercises in imagery or poetry; even as word-pictures and cartoons. How can one recapture for others the experience of the presence of God, overwhelming in his being, awesome in his judgment, heart-breaking in his very offer of forgiveness and love? What words can be found to describe such experiences? How many have themselves known such experiences, so that they may begin to understand the words that are used? The Bible makes its attempts in the

[1] Exodus 21. 24; Leviticus 24. 20; Deuteronomy 19, 21; cf. Matthew 5. 38-39.

stories of Adam and Eve,[1] Moses,[2] Samuel,[3] Isaiah;[4] in the description of the events of the first Whitsuntide,[5] and of St. Paul's conversion,[6] to grapple with the symbolism of the words used and to wrestle with the deep mysteries of confrontation with God, even as Jacob wrestled at the ford of Jabbok.[7] To avoid such a discipline and be content with an exposition on the verbal plain is to miss the wealth of biblical imagery and poetic insight which is the mark of true inspiration.

Yet children, at least up to the age of ten or eleven, are literally-minded and possess only a simple kind of logic. Attempts to explain the inner meaning of the stories are largely lost on them and they can only make their own guesses at explanation. It is this reason, among others, that has led Dr. Goldman to refer to the Bible as a 'difficult book' and one that ought not to be offered to children without sensible safeguards.

In the fourth place, there is an urgent need for Christian teachers to be aware of their true priorities. At a time when so few people, young or old, come from Christian homes, nothing can be taken for granted. In Great Britain, as in so many other parts of the world, we face a situation of increasing secularism. Nothing less than an earnest endeavour to communicate the Christian faith is good enough. And this is more demanding, more challenging, and in its way more exhilarating than being content to 'teach the Bible'. If today there are those who seem to be relegating the place of the Bible to a secondary position, it is not necessarily because they

[1] Genesis 3. 7–21.
[2] Exodus 3. 1–6.
[3] 1 Samuel 3. 1–10.
[4] Isaiah 6. 1–8.
[5] Acts 2. 1–4.
[6] Acts 9. 1–8.
[7] Genesis 32. 22–32.

F

have little respect for it. It may be, and certainly is in many cases, because they have come to see the mistake of regarding Bible teaching as an end in itself. Such teaching, which may have been good of its kind, has become the enemy of the best.

The Christian faith may be confirmed by the Scriptures as its recognized source of authority, but the faith itself is bigger than its written record. There may be (and I hope to show that this is so) a place for the Bible in the process of Christian education, but it must firmly be acknowledged that it is a means to an end, and not an end in itself. There can be no higher authority for this statement than Christ himself. No one had greater respect for the Scriptures than he, and his frequent references, direct and indirect, bear witness to his knowledge of them. But there is no doubt that he realized their limitations and was aware of the dangers of assuming that they were sufficient by themselves.

Moreover, even when the Scriptures are rightly judged to be a means towards the end of communicating the faith, an undue emphasis upon them may also lead to difficulties. The Newsom Report, discussing the place of Bible-study in religious instruction in secondary schools, asserts that such study is 'itself a difficult literary and historical art, once the simple story-telling stage is over. From this source teachers are expected to build up by inference a general body of Christian teaching. This is to go a very long way round for most of the boys and girls with whom we are concerned, and many of them get lost on the way.'[1]

Most teachers, when they are honest, and not placed on the defensive, will acknowledge that there is some truth in the statements so far made. In practice, if not always in theory, they are compelled to modify their

[1] *Half Our Future* (H.M.S.O.).

position, and to that extent do not teach the Bible as an end in itself. It is not without significance that even among those most committed to Bible-centred teaching there has been a willingness to introduce methods which take away the baldness of approach to Bible study. There is also evidence to suggest that certain 'all-Bible' courses produced from time to time have not been as popular as might be supposed.

It would be a pity, therefore, if the present discussions on the place of the Bible in Christian education led to an increasingly defensive position on the part of some who otherwise might be ready objectively to realign their priorities and re-examine their emphasis. An awareness of the problems in using Bible material should not drive extremists to the point of banishing the Bible altogether, with a consequent reaction in the other direction.

One cannot but be impressed by the numbers of Bibles (or New Testaments, or Gospels) which are sold and distributed throughout the world each year. Nor can one fail to recognize that, beyond the reasoning of man, God is still able somehow to speak through the Scriptures to the condition of man, evoking from him without intermediary guidance the right kind of response. Evidence is at hand, year by year, in the reports of Societies like the British and Foreign Bible Society, which unmistakably confirms that this is so. Educators today are coming increasingly to recognize the part which Bible-study and adult fellowship groups, which sprang up with the Evangelical Revival of the eighteenth century, have played in the adult education movements of this country, and in the development of a society sensitive to moral and social responsibility.

To close the Bible and indicate to ordinary people, young and old, that the Book is too difficult to understand, may seem a retrograde and dangerous step to take. When all the difficulties have been faced, and all the problems recognized, it still remains true that the Word of God seems able to be spoken through the Scriptures even to the simplest of people.

On the other hand, evidence is increasing which seems to suggest that an unthinking readiness, not merely to leave the Bible 'open', but to insist that the Bible must be taught because it is the Bible, can serve to prejudice growing boys and girls, and adults too, from wanting to read the Bible. The paradox of this situation is that the more fervently one demands the Bible to be taught, the less those being taught seems to respond to the truths it contains.

It would seem obvious, therefore, that while one retains the belief that the Bible should be 'open' to all, one should at the same time recognize that this is no justification for insisting that the Bible – as the Bible – should be compulsory reading for all. The Bible, properly used, may still be an authoritative means to an end. But it remains a means towards the end of Christian education and evangelism; it is not the end itself. Too great an insistence upon 'teaching the Bible' may defeat the very purpose for which such teaching is intended.

One cannot gainsay those occasions when the Bible has, from its pages, offered divine illumination to those who accidentally, or providentially, have found themselves reading it. 'The wind blows where it wills, and you hear the sound of it, but you do not know whence it comes or whither it goes.'[1] And this should keep both evangelist and educator humble. But this is no argument for building it into a comprehensive system of education. The spirit of God is more likely to work through the careful and dedicated service of teachers who seek to

[1] John 3. 8.

bring all things under the control of the Holy Spirit than through those who allow the Bible to be open regardless, and hope that somehow, sometime, he will speak to those compelled to read its pages. A much safer guide is found in the encounter of Philip and the eunuch whom he found reading from Isaiah.[1] 'Do you understand what you are reading?' Philip asked. And the reply came back, 'How can I, unless someone guides me?'

The question raised by the eunuch in his conversation with Philip is an important one. Perhaps only in the realms of religious education where authoritative writings are involved is it assumed that the same text-book should be used without modification by the expert scholar and by the youngest learner.

Generally speaking, it is assumed that a text-book is a standard work to which reference may be made by those studying the subject under review. As such, it seeks to correlate the relevant facts and ideas associated with the subject, and its value is recognized in so far as it is comprehensive in such correlation. The subject may be philosophy, or mathematics, or biology, or English literature. The authoritative, or standard, works on these kinds of subjects are usually reserved for the scholars and the specialists, and are rarely read by the ordinary scholar, even if he knows of their existence. The teacher's task is that of interpreting and sharing at simpler levels the subject-matter contained in the reference works or standard text-books. For this purpose, he sometimes uses other more simple text-books, or writes his own for the benefit of those he seeks to teach.

By this process a student may naturally proceed from one grade of knowledge to another, and at each stage the requisite kind of text-book will be available, until

[1] Acts **8.** 26–40.

he, too, is able to read and understand the formative standard works for himself.

In some senses, therefore, it is unfortunate that the Bible has come to be regarded as a text-book. In the process of time it has been divided into 'books' and subdivided into chapters and verses (though these latter divisions are arbitrary and sometimes quite artificial) and by this means it becomes a relatively easy book of reference. But ease of reference alone does not constitute validity of description as a text-book. And, on many counts, it does not fall within the category of standard works of reference.

Its reliability and authority have already been considered, but throughout the Bible has been shown to be, not a correlation of facts and ideas at all, but supremely a book describing life-situations of individuals and communities and races, with all the unevenness of life itself. Moreover, while even a cursory reading is sufficient to show that it is not an easy book to understand there is still the notion that it should be available to all, from the youngest scholar to the wisest specialist.

The place of the Bible in the life of the Church is such that it challenges the concentrated intelligence of the scholars with problems of history and textual criticism, with theological concepts and philosophical ideas.

At the same time, it is placed into the hands of teachers for their own illumination and for the guidance of those in their care. And at the same time the children are encouraged to say, 'Tell me the stories of Jesus' and to take the Bible into their own hands to read every day.

Here, then, is the dilemma which confronts many thinking people at the present time. Is the Bible so difficult a book to understand properly that it is better to regard it as a text-book for the experts only, to be used by them for their own terms of reference, but to be interpreted to others who will use 'simple' text-books, not necessarily based upon the Scriptures but in harmony with biblical truth? Or, because the Bible is an 'open book' won at great cost, is it better for all to be able to read it, even if there is risk of misunderstanding and misinterpretation? Or is there a third alternative which may preserve the essential elements of the other two possibilities? Much of the present debate on the place of the Bible in Christian education really hinges on these possibilities.

The Rev. Alan Dale's excellent Bible translations[1] are an attempt to overcome the language problems which children have in reading the Bible, but other problems relating to literalism and symbolism remain. And, of course, there are vast areas of the Bible which are not included in Dale's translations, about which there might be doubtful value in seeking to work out such translations.

Only when serious efforts are made to re-think the positive place of the Bible in schemes of Christian education, and to show their validity and importance, can the way ahead be properly discerned. The eunuch was surely right in putting his question to Philip. How can we understand the Scriptures unless someone will guide us? It is to this aspect of our study that we must now turn.

[1] *New World, Vols.* 1–5 by Alan T. Dale (Oxford University Press), 1966.

7

THE PRESENT POSITION

IN the last chapter we examined some of the factors which help us to see that the teaching of Bible material is not as easy or straightforward as some might suppose. The fact has to be faced, however, that even if the difficulties can be overcome by a proper understanding of the ways in which the Bible may be used, these difficulties can still arise from sources beyond our control. No educational influence can exist in isolation from others, whether it be home, day school, or church. And no form of protection can insulate those growing up today from the influences of their social environment.

My own discussions on this subject with teachers have often led us to see that even if every care is taken not to introduce certain Bible stories to an age-group unsuitable to receive them, they will probably hear of them from elsewhere. Bible picture-books, story-books of the Bible, lessons taught in other places, the Bible itself as an open book; all these make it hard for one with strong views about the suitability or otherwise of selected passages from the Scriptures.

It is impossible to guard against every kind of circumstance, nor can we imagine ideal situations in which there is perfect harmony of understanding among those most vitally concerned. With the best care in the world, there will be children who will assume the Bible to be a special book, a magic book, God's book; a book where everything in it is absolutely and literally true.

There will also be those who will reject it out of hand because someone has said somewhere that science has disproved it, and it is really a collection of 'fairy-tales' in which churches and parsons have a vested interest!

Teachers, in these situations, can only do their best. But it is important for them to realize that nothing less than the best will be good enough. Two qualities, it seems to me, are essential, and much else that can and ought to be done in the use of Bible material follows upon them.

In the first place, teachers must be capable of showing that reconciliation is possible between the statements and ideas which are to be found within the Bible itself, and those which are revealed when the Bible view of the world is set alongside the modern view of the world. This does not mean that, at every stage of a child's development or on every occasion when questions are asked, teachers should be expected to hold detailed discussions such as appear in earlier chapters of this book. It does mean that at the proper time, and in simple terms, the right attitude towards the Bible – what it is and what it does not pretend to be – will be encouraged. One of the needs of our time is a restoration of confidence in the reliability and authority of the Bible as we now understand these qualities, and if is often too late to build up such confidence when so much has to be re-taught and so many misconceptions corrected.

The ability of teachers to encourage the right attitude to the Bible is basic, because only when children have reached the age when they begin to reason things out for themselves can special teaching-courses on the structure of the Bible and its place in the Christian view of life be offered. Yet their general conception of the Bible will already have taken shape in the years before, when specific lessons on the Bible may have been given in a way inappropriate for their age.

It is becoming increasingly clear that many foundations for life, in all its ranges, are established in the
early years. Social relationships, the reality of security
and love, attitudes to sex, the quest for knowledge –
these are formed long before there can be intellectual
discussions about them. The same must become true of
the Bible itself. Everything that can be done should be
done to ensure that no false claims about the Bible
are made, and that the proper respect for its place in
the Christian life is not founded upon anything which
later cannot be sustained.

In the second place, teachers must develop the art or
the skill of making the Bible world relevant to the
twentieth-century. Life that revolves around sand and
sandals, sheep and goats, nomadic tribes and rural
communities, is very different from life that is judged in
terms of space research, atomic power, computers and
technology, commerce and industry. And it is not enough
to be content with superficial translations of the words
and external circumstances of the scriptural records.
Indeed, the greater the emphasis upon verbalism, the
more remote and irrelevant the Bible becomes.

The key to the kind of translation that is required is
to be found in the universality of human experience.
Human nature being what it is the experiences of men
are much the same in every age and place. The outward
circumstances, the external contexts, may differ very
much from one century to another and from one part of
the world to another. The inner thoughts and feelings
and responses of people remain constant.

It is just because this is so that the Bible comes into
its own. God has ordained that his truth shall be revealed
in the records of the life-situations of individual men
and of communities. And once we begin to examine the
Bible to see what kind of experiences made up their

lives, we can then put such experiences side by side with similar experiences in modern life.

The needs of men are needs which emerge out of the life he lives, and God becomes real as those needs are properly met. The human needs of companionship, of sympathy, of understanding; the experiences of failure and frustration, of pain and suffering; the challenges implicit in a search for fulfilment and wholeness; these are familiar to us all. And every one has its parallel in the Bible records. It is in these experiences that God meets us just as he met people in days gone by.

And what can be said of individuals may also be said of the corporate experiences of the community. There are problems of racial distinction and of under-developed countries; situations of political intrigue and economic manoeuvre; there is the fear of war and rumour of war. It is in such encounters that God can become real for the world of men, just as he became real to those people whose stories are told in the Scriptures.

The Bible may not be an infallible authority, throwing up the right text for the right occasion. But because it is uniquely the book which unfolds God's purposes for men through the actual experiences of men, as indivi-duals and in their relation to one another, it is possible for it to speak to the present generation pertinently and effectively. But this is only achieved when we learn the art of setting our experiences alongside the parallel biblical experiences. The external circumstances of modern life may be different from those of life in the Bible, but the experiences of men themselves are the same.

So in Christian education it is important to bring to light the experiences of those whom we teach and put them side by side with biblical passages which, when studied in depth, reveal the same experiences.

By using the Bible in this way, one can begin to see the importance of the whole Bible record, dealing, as it does, with failure as well as success, with sin as well as salvation. A book purged of all references to human weakness, offering a stylized picture of artificial perfection, far from being an authority for the religious way of life, would defeat such ends. It is precisely because it shows men misunderstanding God and rebelling against him, as well as finding peace and joy in their acceptance of his will, that it remains an authority to which one can turn with confidence.

Once teachers are able to feed into the minds and imaginations the right ideas about the Bible, and its relevance in terms of experience, it is possible to consider the principles on which the selection of Bible material ought to be based. Christian education is concerned with people who are necessarily at different stages of development, and while we may recognize the importance of parallelism of experience, we must also recognize that similar experiences take different forms at different stages of development.

A primary child is very different from a young adult, and the junior from the parent. The parallelism of experience must, therefore, always be valid for the people receiving instruction, and must not range so far beyond the immediacy of experience as to be incomprehensible.

For example, the experiences of temptation come to all of us, young and old. But the ways in which the temptations come differ from one person to another. The selection of Bible material needs to take account of this factor, so that, so far as circumstances allow, what is chosen is in accordance with the changing and developing needs of those whom we teach.

From this process of taking every aspect of Christian truth and relevant Bible material stage by stage with the natural development of boys and girls, we can overcome the danger of seeking to teach too much too quickly. Aspects of religious truth, even stories or parables, ought not to be introduced before they can be properly appreciated. This is not to say that a time will ever come when they will be fully understood, for it is part of the inspirational value of the Scriptures that no one can ever claim that he now knows all there is to know about them. It is rather to say that some aspects are blunted in their sharpness, and spoiled of their effectiveness, if they are offered prematurely.

Moreover, there is also the danger that, because they are not properly understood, they may, indeed, be actually misunderstood. Some teachers, taking a superficial view of parallelism of experience, have assumed that stories of babies and small children must inevitably appeal to the young. So they have told the stories of the infant Moses or Samuel,[1] and have been surprised when the children have failed to appreciate their meaning. In some cases the children have become worried about being left alone or have imagined their name being called out in the darkness of their bedroom at night.

It is clear, therefore, that a more careful selection of Bible material needs to be made if it is to be effective and relevant. Parallelism of experience, applied in terms of natural development, may offer general guidance, but is there anything that should be added? In recent years this subject has received much close attention and we can now indicate more precisely on what principles selection may properly be made.

Many of us have supposed that, because junior boys

[1] cf. Exodus 2. 1–10; 1 Samuel 3. 1–10.

and girls respond to stories of adventure, it is a good thing to introduce them to some of the adventures contained in Old Testament passages. We have also rationalized this process by assuming that, just as they accept cowboys and Indians, cops and robbers, they will also accept the biblical stories, taking from them the right kind of moral and discarding the rest.

Unfortunately, Bible stories are taken from a book they are taught to believe is 'different'. Unlike cowboys and Indians, these stories are 'real'. Moreover, the context in which they are taught is often that of Christan worship; worship which is imaginative, sensitive and effective. Thus, the response to the story is very different from that to other stories. Without always being aware of it, the children imbibe concepts of God which are not only anthropomorphic, but, much more dangerously, are in direct contradiction to those offered by Christ's revelation of God and his teaching about God, as it is found in the New Testament.

Junior boys and girls may well respond to the stories of the poor outnumbered Israelites vanquishing the hosts of the powerful enemy; they may well begin to feel that here is the vindication of the principle of right overcoming might. But at the same time they will come to accept a view of God who encourages slaughter and battle, destruction and death, in order to prove his supremacy. This is far removed from the picture of God revealed in Christ.

We must ensure that whatever is referred to in Bible material, whether in Old or New Testaments, must be capable of relating to Christian interpretation. Only at an age when boys and girls are able to grapple with the general principles of historical development of thought should they be confronted with parts of the Bible which illustrate those principles. And it is here that what has already been said about the unity of the Bible with Christ himself as the key to that unity becomes relevant.

Selection of Bible material may also be based upon a thematic approach to the Scriptures, always recognizing that the items themselves are within the experiences of those to whom they are introduced. Reference has been made to Alan Dale's New Testament Translations.[1] It is unfair to his work to suggest that it is based solely upon a concern for using language that can be understood by children. Of equal significance is the way in which he brings his selected material together, in order to illustrate certain items within the experiences of the children themselves. Other experiments in a thematic approach have been made,[2] which take important symbols of Biblical language, and help boys and girls to explore them, so that they can feel for themselves the experiential and spiritual significance which underlies them.

Enough has been written to indicate that, far from ignoring the Bible or denigrating it because of the genuine difficulties which exist in its presentation, we give it a very important place. It should not be supposed, however, that the Bible only exists in order that it may be taught. It may well be that the discussion so far could have given the impression that the Bible is to be regarded as a kind of work of reference, to be incorporated only after careful thought into a syllabus of teaching.

Christian education is, however, incomplete unless time is found for the experience of Christian worship. This is obviously recognized in the life of the Church and its Junior Church departments; it is also recognized

---

[1] See p. 87.

[2] cf. *The Importance of Bread* by Margaret E. Hughes; *Sheep and Shepherds* by R. Dingwall (Rupert Hart-Davis Educational Publications).

to some extent in the concern for Assemblies of Worship in day-schools. Within such a context of worship one naturally thinks of the Scriptures as the basis for selected readings. And it is within the ordering of worship that the Bible may most effectively be used. One can afford to risk the selection of passages which may not be understood in all their detail, but which carry something of the majesty and poetry and vision of inspired writing. The words of the prophet, splendid and awful; the praises of the psalmist, lifting up the heart, and quickening the imagination; the declarations of the Apostle, challenging and inspiring; these often stand in their own right as expressions of God's offers to men and the responses of men to God which form the heart and soul of Christian worship.

If there is a place in study for the botanist, there is also a place in life for the poet. There are times when it is necessary to analyse, but there are also times when 'we murder to dissect'. We ought not to assume that all the time we should be using the Bible, dissecting its meaning, referring to it as though it clinched all arguments. Within worship, we can let it speak for itself. And this, in the end, may be more effective than all our teaching.

PART THREE

THE BIBLE FOR THOSE WE TEACH

8

YOUNG CHILDREN

Two factors of paramount importance for a proper understanding of young children must be borne in mind all the time, both of which are relevant to a study of Christian Education and the Bible. They are admirably summed up for us in the words, 'It cannot be emphasized too strongly that the first seven years of life are the most important for the religious development of the child, and that in these seven years he is not capable of religious experience in the sense in which the adult understands it.'[1] This statement makes it abundantly clear that no one should underestimate the need for imaginative and sensitive care in bringing good influences to bear upon children in these early and formative years. At the same time it reminds us that we have no right to expect such children to understand intellectual verbalizations about the Bible and the Christian faith, or religion as such, and that the kind of distinctions adults make about the sacred and the secular have no validity in their experience.

Despite the emphases which educationalists and psychologists have made in their assessments of the influences of early years which affect us all, society has been slow to learn their lessons. Only now, with the great increase in juvenile delinquency and the emergence of problem children, and with the need to find causes of imbalance in the attitudes and behaviour of

---

[1] *Your Growing Child and Religion* by R. G. Lee (Pelican), 1963.

adults, is more attention being given to the subject of child care in the wider sense of that phrase.

If we sometimes find it difficult to understand why some boys and girls seem able to respond easily to Christian truth, while others find it just as easy to reject it, the reasons are seldom to be found in syllabuses of religious education or personalities of leaders and teachers. They are to be found more often in the circumstances of life which go back to early childhood. Embedded in the experiences of these years are the fundamental lessons, for good or ill, which have been learned about life. Influences for good which may be brought to bear upon the children are correspondingly weaker or stronger according to the kind of lessons imbibed in those early years.

The adult world may well be able to discuss at an academic level distinctions between love and hatred, aggression and fear, guilt and forgiveness, security and anxiety, but long before boys and girls can rationalise their thoughts about these different attitudes and experiences, they have themselves received them into their personalities. A preparedness to reject a way of life built upon hatred and violence; a willingness to accept a way of life based upon love and forgiveness; these depend much less upon our skills as moral and spiritual teachers than we sometimes imagine. They spring from lessons learned before any 'lessons' were consciously taught.

For this reason the first concern of parents and teachers is not to teach articulated truths, but to surround their children with 'such things as are pure and true, lovely and of good report'.[1] Only by doing so will a religious interpretation of life make sense at a time when it is possible for interpretations about life to be

[1] *Order of Service for the Baptism of Infants* (Methodist Book of Offices).

made. 'The aim of religious education is not to constrain the child to become religious, but to ensure that as he comes to maturity of development he will find in religion the fullest expression of his inward self.'[1]

One cannot discuss here the full implications of this notion of child psychology. But it has obvious references to the way in which the Bible may or may not be used with young children. There have been occasions when at the end of a lecture or conference, parents have come to talk to me privately about their children. How proud they have sometimes been because their offspring have learned to recite a Bible passage! Is not this an indication of their growing spiritual discernment? And, as the parents have been quick to point out, the children have obviously enjoyed the exercise.

We have to note, therefore, that within the experience of the children, the ability to quote the Scriptures – however simply – and the keenness to learn the Scriptures, is not by itself a sign of spiritual development. It is almost certainly due to a desire to please the parents, and whether it be a nursery rhyme, or a stringing together of swear words (which I have known in a certain colliery district!), or a Bible passage, the words and their meanings have been far less important than the effect upon their parents. It cannot be assumed that the best way to train a child in religious matters is to introduce him to the recognized forms of worship – prayer, Bible stories, and hymns.

This is not to say, of course, that it does not matter whether a child is told a Bible story or a jingle of rhyming slang. It is to say that the child does not possess the intellectual capacity to understand what is being learned and that the motive for learning is not religious or irreligious, but simply wanting to do what will please

[1] R. G. Lee , op. cit.

the parents. It is also to say that it is the attitude of the parents, and, a little later, the teachers, which is of paramount importance. The naturalness of their own prayer-life, the acceptance of the Bible as a book worthy of respect, the ease with which they can refer to God, these are more helpful for the growing child than talks about prayer, lessons on the Bible, discourses about God. The child will accept the former as being natural to life; he will be inclined to reject the latter as impositions or unnatural lessons which for some reason the adults think it is good for him to learn.

There is, however, a more fundamental aspect of life for growing children which has relevance to what is taught from the Bible. The experience of the vast majority is an experience of love and security stemming almost entirely from a mother's care and a father's protection. We know that not all homes are all that they should be. Indeed, the best parents are most aware of their failures and shortcomings. But genuine love has a habit of overriding mistakes, and this remains true in far more homes than moralists sometimes acknowledge. For young children, therefore, the sense of care and protection which is part of their experience can and ought to be widened to a realization of God's fatherly care and protection. This, it seems to me, is more useful than the prevailing emphasis upon Jesus as Friend.

An association between the biblical record of God as our father and the experience of home life is important because although many children go through the stage of confusing their own father with God as father, the need to be emancipated from a father-fixation has long been recognized by psychologists, and this can be done most easily and naturally when the notion of God as father is clearly established. Freud was very perceptive in his diagnosis of this father–child relationship and the dangers inherent in it. He was far wider from the mark in his attempts to draw from it the cause and reason for Christian belief. For Christianity, properly understood, is not an extension of Freud's 'Oedipus Complex', it is the answer to it. If this crisis in the development of children is to be overcome, it is most likely to be achieved by an early awareness of God revealed as father.[1]

This view has been well expressed by Dr. Bovet who made the distinction between the 'paternalization of God' and the 'divinization of parents', and who has helped us to 'see in filial adoration the prototype of religious feelings and the origin of theological dogmas.'[2]

Perhaps the key to this kind of emancipation is to be found again in the biblical conception of God, who is not merely father, but a special kind of father, awesome and majestic, who loves and is loved, but with whom one can never be on familiar terms. My colleague, the Rev. C. D. Bacon, quotes a four-year-old, looking up at the stars in the night sky, who is impelled suddenly to exclaim, 'God must be a-a-a magic man!'[3] To introduce to small children, particularly in worship, those references to God as father and creator, is not to move outside their experience. It is to use their experience and enable them to come to terms with their own home relationships, and a beginning of a relationship with one who is both within the home-life and outside it.

Throughout these pages there have been constant references to the Bible as a book about life. All experience is impregnated with the presence and purpose of God. This, too, is important for young children. The world of work and play, of hours of employment and

[1] cf. R. G. Lee, op. cit.
[2] Quoted by B. A. Yeaxlee in *Religion and the Growing Mind* (Nisbet), 1939.
[3] *Growing Up* by C. D. Bacon (M.Y.D.).

leisure, with their hard divisions, and clear-cut rules and regulations, does not exist for children. All life is a process of learning. 'For the young child play is the serious business of the day. Play is the means by which a child tackles the world about him, and the way in which he prepares for the life that lies ahead.'[1]

It is a pity that such a wholeness of life is rarely retained beyond childhood, for this is precisely what the Bible seeks to reveal. We must be sure that this view is communicated to the children so that they may come to appreciate God as father and creator who shares in all life, in all society, in all that they are seeking to understand and appreciate about life.

Reference must obviously be made to the enjoyment children find in listening to stories and having them repeated again and again. Indeed, it will be the experience of most parents and teachers that so carefully are the stories followed that even the slightest deviation or alteration in forms of words will be immediately detected. There is no reason why Bible stories should not be included in the repertoire; but again we must remember that the response will be exactly the same as with any other story. It will not be different because it happens to come from the Bible.

Such stories will include elements in the life of Jesus, a selection of the stories he himself told, and some account of the great heroes of religion. 'But they must be left to absorb the stories in their own way and make their own selection of what is relevant to life.'[2] Attempts to moralize or indoctrinate will defeat our purpose and may, sooner or later, help to create barriers of resistance to the very insights into life which those stories might otherwise reveal.

[1] C. D. Bacon, op. cit.
[2] R. G. Lee, op. cit.

From three and a half years onwards the vocabulary of children widens considerably, and some teachers estimate that during the fourth year a vocabulary can in fact be doubled. This is a natural phenomenon in development, and it is noted for two reasons.

In the first place children need to be able to relate experience and situations to words in order to identify them in their own thinking, to share them with others and to begin a processs of linking one experience with another. In the second place, children need to articulate or to give expression to their feelings and attitudes as they become involved in experiences and situations.

There are some who contend that teaching by involvement is sufficient in itself, and that any attempt to put words to experience is to defeat the purpose of the experience and to return to a verbalized form of teaching. For the reasons given in the previous paragraph I do not agree that the putting of words alongside experiences is unnecessary. On the contrary there is nothing so pathetic as the sight of a child wanting to communicate and being frustrated to the point of anger because no words are known to express what is felt. But how we delight in children who are finding the words – if sometimes the wrong words – to share with others their own discoveries and interests.

We do not wish by the use of the Bible to burden a child's mind with abstract theological terms, but we can encourage a growth of vocabulary and an identification of experience by the use of simple Bible phrases, in worship and in story-telling. And this should certainly be done.

Finally, it is possible to use the Bible in the thematic sense which has been discussed in earlier chapters. Themes chosen for this purpose will be related to the natural interests of the children themselves, their homes and their schools; their companions and those whom they are led to trust because they help them; their growing awareness of the world about them. These can and ought to be explored and enacted, and they have their parallels in Bible themes. Care, however, needs to be exercised lest there is an artificiality in an ostentatious or deliberate turning to the Bible, as though the Bible belonged to a different world from that of the children.

The home-life of Jesus; Jesus the helper; God the provider and protector; such themes can be introduced to those of four to seven years of age. But they must retain their simplicity and should be introduced naturally into other aspects of the theme, and certainly not imposed as a lesson to be learned. It is the interweaving of the threads of everyday experience with parallel 'Bible' experiences, so that there is a wholeness of appreciation, that matters. The sincere but misguided attempts by teachers or parents to draw out morals or make distinctions between the everyday and the Bible can only serve to confuse. And in some cases may set up barriers which afterwards need to be broken down.

So far we have thought about the Bible in terms of relevant material available for helping young children in their growing life. Just as the most important factor is not the material itself, however, but the warmth of love and genuiness of care which really matters, so when we think of teaching about the Bible, it is the attitude of the teachers and parents themselves which matters most.

There is no place for formal teaching about the Bible among young children. But there will obviously be references to the Bible from time to time. And the natural desire on the part of teachers to be simple can have its dangers. There can be a tendency to refer to the

Bible as 'God's book' and this can so easily lead to a false conception of the Bible. References to the Bible itself should therefore be kept to a minimum, and there is no reason why attempts to be simple should lead to an avoidance of reference to the Bible as the Bible.

Children may want to know 'What is the Bible' Or they may build up an image of what they think the Bible is. It is therefore equally important to define it as a book which tells us about God. Not 'God's book', as though he had written it word for word; but a book to which we turn to help us know more about God.

It is a good thing to have an attractively-bound copy of the Bible, and not a sombre black volume. It is also a good thing for it to be an illustrated edition, so that if children ask to see it they are not confronted with small black type which goes on from page to page. Some of the simple projects which may be encouraged can be the building up of 'picture-books' related to Bible stories. Work of this kind is of more value than many printed versions of illustrated Bible stories for children, which often select Old Testament material unsuitable for those of that age.

Choice of material in story-telling, in themes, in worship; references to the Bible itself and the copies of the Bible in use; all these need to be considered so that children will not have wrong conceptions of the Bible, but will have, within the limits of their experience, an appreciation of a book which they enjoy and which confirms their awareness of love and security in a world which daily becomes wider and sometimes more frightening.

9

BOYS AND GIRLS

LIP-SERVICE is often paid to the fact that every age in the development of human life brings with it its own peculiar problems. In practice, however, there has been too facile an acceptance of the idea that boys and girls who have grown out of the childhood years but have not yet reached adolescence are most straightforward and free from psychological complexities. It is true that junior boys and girls go through a period of the consolidation of their powers and reflect a natural balance between mind and body which is only retained with disciplined effort later in life. It is equally true that they often give an appearance of uncomplicated extroverts, noisy and boisterous, and easily satisfied if their energies can be rightly directed. It should not be assumed, however, that they do not need sensitive and careful handling. And certainly, in their Christian education, more thought needs to be devoted to their needs than has hitherto been the case. It is not for nothing that the junior age-range is the period when attendance at Church and Sunday School comes most strongly to be resisted.

We cannot consider here the full implications of this in terms of Church policy; they are dealt with in the wider context of Church programmes for boys and girls. But the challenge to re-think the presentation of the Bible to this age range is inescapable, and there is much still to be learned.

In some ways the transition from the approach to

young children to that to growing boys and girls is made too sharply and too strongly. In other ways, however, there is insufficient attention paid to the fact that juniors cannot be treated as if they were little children. Nowhere is this more so than in the selection of story material. The art of story-telling is basic to any teacher, whatever age-range is under review, and there is a readiness to appreciate that the methods employed must differ according to the age-range. It is in the choice of story to be told where greatest care needs to be exercised.

One of the outstanding differences between children and juniors is in their attitude to stories. The junior, who is moving into a realistic or literalist age, is at the same time expressing his rejection of fairy-tales. These belong to the age of childhood and he has grown out of that. Moreover, while the child enjoys the repetition of stories, the junior is only too ready to express contempt for stories he has already heard.[1]

It is for this reason that the number of Bible stories told to small children should be limited. An over-exposure to Bible stories at that stage serves only to create difficulties at the second stage. More seriously, there emerges the problem of interpreting the stories. An unwise selection of Biblical material may lead to rejection because it is associated with fairy-tales and is therefore 'kids' stuff' to be ignored or abandoned. This, as Dr. Goldman has clearly shown, is fraught with danger and misunderstanding.

Boys and girls, Dr. Goldman writes, develop a 'tendency to focus upon trivialities of the story. And this can give rise to arrested development in that his own childish explanations lead him to believe that he does

[1] cf. *The Development of Religious Experience in Children* by E. Harris (1944).

not need to think more deeply about the story.'[1]

Before we reach any conclusions about a right selection of Bible stories, however, it is necessary to consider another factor in the experience of growing boys and girls. The co-ordination of mental and physical factors allied to the period of the consolidation of powers provide them with a spirit of independence. They are drawn increasingly into the world of their contemporaries, are happy to be away from the security of home and school environment, and are ready to assert their existence in their own right. It is this which attracts them to adventures of all kinds, and makes them eager to respond to challenges which give them the opportunities to prove themselves.

For this reason it is natural to select Bible stories which illustrate adventure and excitement and the willingness to face all the odds out of loyalty to what is believed to be the right. Unfortunately, such Bible material has too often been presented in a literal fashion from the Bible itself, or has been given in such detail as to encourage the reading of the story from the Bible, and this has raised many problems of interpretation. And when this has happened the fears of Dr. Goldman have been realized.

Many readers will be familiar with the two Bible stories used by Dr. Goldman in his research, which relate to the deliverance of the Israelites out of the hands of the Egyptians. The one refers to Moses and the Burning Bush,[2] and the other to the Crossing of the Red Sea.[3] It is probably true that if such stories are told literally, or as stories in their own right, the boys and girls are given such detail that they must inevitably draw their own conclusions. They will either regard

[1] Dr. R. Goldman, op. cit.
[2] Exodus 3. 1–6. [3] Exodus 14.

them as fairy-tales or draw their own childish logical conclusions about the ways in which the stories might have been real. And the teacher who wishes to overcome these obstacles will be drawn into explanations outside the understanding of the boys and girls.

Does this mean, then, that such a thrilling story as the deliverance of the Israelites under the leadership of Moses should not be told? If the answer is 'No', we have to accept the view that the Old Testament should virtually be ignored. But we need not answer the question in the negative if we are prepared to release ourselves from a detailed re-telling of the Bible material, chapter by chapter, or event by event; and, instead, are prepared to relate the main outline of the whole story, at the same time giving a reasonable account of those elements in the story which cause difficulties when read from the Bible itself.

This point was made in a critical comment on Dr. Goldman's research by Gordon K. Hawes, and insufficient attention has been paid to it. Writing in *Learning for Living*,[1] he said that to isolate such stories as Moses and the Burning Bush or the Crossing of the Red Sea from the wider context of the whole adventure of dedication to leadership and deliverance from an oppressor 'is to do violence to the whole principle of true biblical interpretation.'

A right approach is, of course, only possible, if one's attitude to the Bible is right. The fundamentalist may not be prepared to do it, and must risk the consequences. But given a reasonable approach, most of the difficulties about literal interpretation will be overcome without – at the stage of junior boys and girls – having to be raised. And a positive approach to Bible truth will be achieved.

[1] '(Mis)leading Questions' in *Learning for Living*, March 1965.

It is also only possible if the teacher has the skill to tell the story imaginatively and with understanding, and can adhere to the main facts (which biblical scholarship can support) and bring interpretation to bear upon other aspects of the story (for which there is no historical foundation).

Behind the discussion on Bible material as a basis for story-telling lies a more fundamental question. Why is the story being told? If the purpose is to teach the Bible there must be the inevitable temptation to go into the kind of details which makes the material unsuitable. But if the stories are related to themes, then there is again a release from the imprisonment of textual Bible teaching.

I have referred to the sense of adventure to which juniors readily respond. The Bible abounds in themes which can be related to the experiences of modern life and which can effectively be offered in a syllabus for the junior age-range. 'God calls us into the Unknown'; 'The God who delivers'; 'In search of right and wrong', give tremendous scope for boys and girls, and enable Bible stories to be used in the broad sweep of Israelite history. These themes are freed from literal interpretation or childishly anthropomorphic views of God, and do not depend upon the teaching of biblical history for its own sake.

We have much to learn from modern research, and we need to discipline ourselves accordingly. But we do not need to panic, and assume that the Bible is unsuitable. It is only unsuitable when we adhere too closely to a verbalistic plane: once we get beneath to the experiences of the people we can reach the heart of the Bible truth with its invigorating challenge to adventure with God.

The suggestion of a theme like 'In search of right and

wrong' may be linked with the growing sense of justice and fair play which is so strong a characteristic of junior boys and girls. But it can be valid for another reason. Dr. Cattell has pointed out that by the age of seven most children have acquired by imitation, or through the fear of loss of parental affection, or through an anxiety not to displease friends or teachers, a sense of guilt and therefore the beginnings of a notion of sin.[1]

Some psychologists would affirm that such an awareness is a conditional state brought about by the conventions of home life or the society in which the home is placed. It is important to note, therefore, that even in a young boy or girl there is a distinction 'between a false sense of guilt due to mere convention and a genuine one which is a matter of relationship.'[2] That some religious teachers and preachers have not always recognized the distinction, and, indeed, have sometimes themselves blurred the distinctions, does not affect the importance of this truth.

There is no doubt that many children experience for themselves the apparent injustices of parents and yet have the capacity to forgive their parents when they feel that such parents really love and care for them. Neither can it be doubted that when children have offended against their parents guilt can only be removed when forgiveness is offered. These experiences go beneath the acceptance or rejection of conventional behaviour or standards of conduct. They lie at the heart of relationships, unaffected by outward circumstances or social orthodoxy.

If, therefore, the child needs to know that God is a father who creates and gives care and protection, the junior boys and girls need to know something of a

---

[1] cf. *Psychology and the Religious Quest* by Dr. Cattell.
[2] B. Yeaxlee, op. cit.

father who forgives, and that forgiveness is not a sign of weakness, but of strength. Awareness of right and wrong, truth and falsehood, may seem rigid in the minds of boys and girls, but there is equal need to indicate that failure is not the end. A new start can be made when the rigid standard has not been kept.

Experimental discussions with boys and girls on the subject of 'right and wrong' reveal a tendency to see these areas of life in clear-cut divisions, and their harshness of judgment and punishment, when it affects wrongdoers other than themselves, is well known. There has, therefore, been a tendency – perhaps unconsciously present – to accept this attitude in the selection of Bible material. Boys and girls may well respond to some Old Testament concepts of justice, without being made aware that such concepts were part of the evolution of moral conviction. The teachings of Jesus become an important factor in helping them to go beyond the rigidity of legalism into the realms of compassion and forgiveness. This is important for themselves, as they feel guilty for their own breakdown in right relationships, and in their attitude to others whom they believe have done wrong.

Granted that there is such a need, one can see that the stories (or teachings) of Jesus, and the main events of his life offered to young children (in story form) can begin to be filled out with a measure of interpretive material. What Jesus said and did begins to be broadened out to some understanding of why he said what he did, and why he acted as he did.

One can now turn naturally to another aspect of the psychology of boys and girls. The questions 'What?' and 'Why?' – which are common among growing children – move into the deeper question of 'How?' The apparent literal-mindedness of juniors is reflected in the curiosity which is caused about everything in life. Their expanding knowledge may satisfy their need to know what things are, and what they are for, but they now also want to know how they have become what they are and what makes them work.

It is at this stage of their development that boys and girls exhibit 'a very characteristic and spontaneous outburst of metaphysical curiosity; speculations regarding the origin of things, the first men, the creation of the world and of God himself ... and it is necessary to see in this a crisis, at once intellectual and moral, comparable in many aspects to the crisis of adolescence'[1]

From eight years of age onwards children are progressively introduced to the scientific interpretations of life, in its beginnings and its continuing existence. Whatever view about the Bible, and the early chapters of Genesis, we may have – and this has been discussed earlier in this book – we have to reckon with the fact that, by the time such children have reached the age of eleven, only about half are prepared to accept that the Bible is literally true. And by the time the early period of adolescence has been passed (at about fifteen years of age) only about 5 per cent still accept the Bible as being literally true. These figures are based on Dr. Goldman's analysis, but can be confirmed, negatively and positively in most Sunday School situations. It is important for us to take note of the conclusion reached by Dr. Goldman! 'The child's literalism regarding the Bible may be protracted for too long by teachers and clergy who fear to introduce critical ideas about the Bible to the young.'[2]

Many of the difficulties can be overcome if the right foundations have been laid in references to the Bible while the children are young. But older boys and girls

[1] *The Child's Religion* by Bovet.
[2] Op. cit.

have reached the stage when they can read easily for themselves, and the Bible is an 'open' book. It needs to be made clear that the writers of the early chapters of Genesis were men who put their own construction on the way in which God created and sustains the universe; today, because of our increased knowledge, we can put different constructions on these matters without denying that God is the source and ground of all that lives and moves and has its being.

Once more it is the attitude of the teacher which matters, together with an ability to deal with questions which lie at the back of the minds of the pupils at the level of their understanding. The childish logic which gives rise to difficulties if children have already been conditioned to the literal view of Bible truth can be turned to an advantage if they have already received the notion that the Bible is a book about God, the truths of which are imaginative and poetic, as well as factual.

Those sections of the Bible, and particularly those parts of the Old Testament, which deal with creation, ought not to be studied in their own right – opening up all kinds of problems difficult to handle; instead, they should be used as poetic expressions of the deeper truths of creation we wish to communicate. It is here that one sees the importance of using Bible material as I believe God intends it to be used, and not as an end in itself.

If we take the basic questions of 'What?', 'Why?' and 'How?', and relate them to the Bible itself and the experiences of boys and girls, there is no reason why the right foundations of a growing appreciation of the Bible cannot be established without a process of unlearning having to be undertaken at a later stage. The difficulty of doing this has often been found to be that too much detail is assumed to be necessary. It is this which takes a syllabus of this kind out of the range of the understanding of the children. But the avoidance of the difficulty has led equally often to a position of retarding the development of a right understanding. And in the end boys and girls have assumed the Bible to be just a lot of fairy-tales, or a book which cannot stand the tests of modern knowledge.

There is urgent need, quite apart from a right selection of Bible material, to raise with boys and girls the fundamental questions, 'What is the Bible?', 'Why is it important?', 'How did it come to be written?'. Direct and honest answers to these questions could do much to break through the present problems of the Bible in Christian education. And this can be done imaginatively by encouraging the natural curiosity which is a characteristic of the age.

It would be quite wrong to write this chapter without reference to the place of the Bible in worship and private devotions. The recognition of the place of the Bible in forms of worship is, of course, as valid for juniors as for younger children, and there is no need to repeat here what has been said in the previous chapter. But for juniors there is value in encouraging the corporate reading of selected passages (as distinct from listening to a Bible lesson), and a number of publications are available which give guidance to those responsible for children's assemblies and corporate acts of worship.[1]

More thought needs to be given, however, to the use of the Bible in the encouragement of a personal devotional life. Surrounded by the right kind of influences, many boys and girls wish to continue a practice which may have begun in their earliest years. But they will also want to be more independent, and develop their own practice of some kind of devotional exercise

[1] cf. *Junior Worship* by E. H. Hayes and J. K. Meir (R.E.P.), 1956.

before going to sleep at night. Here I am not concerned with the promotion of such a practice, nor with the many practical problems which arise in different home circumstances; I can only offer comments about the selection of Bible material which may be available for boys and girls who seek to practise, in one way or another, a regular devotional life.

All that has been written already, here and elsewhere, about the principles of selection needs, of course, to be borne in mind. And there is an obvious value in guiding boys and girls so that what they read day by day will be complementary to a syllabus which may be used in their church life. What is supremely important, however, is that they should be helped to develop a right attitude towards the Bible. Every attempt should be made to counteract the idea that the Bible is telling us what is true and what we ought to do, and to introduce the view that life offers to us all kinds of experiences which we need to understand, and the Bible can give us a clue to a proper understanding of these experiences.

Selected Bible readings, however sponsored, should assess the experiences of boys and girls in terms of themes perhaps lasting only a week at a time, so that at the end of the week there will be a true appreciation of the experiences and what God has been able to teach them, through the Bible, about those experiences. Questions need to be posed, rather than answers given, about the passages selected, so that the initiative remains with the reader, and whatever answers emerge become the right answers for him. Such an approach may seem to be hazardous, and less safe than providing the 'right' answers. In terms of true spiritual development, however, and in a worthy recognition of the work of the Holy Spirit, it is likely to produce much better results.

Finally, one needs to recognize that within and beyond these various emphases in Bible teaching, there is at this time of development among boys and girls a ready response to leadership which evokes respect and loyalty. Jesus Christ becomes one in whom they can repose trust, and if in earlier life there has been an emphasis upon the Father, it is now that a clear picture of Jesus should be drawn.

If the purpose of Christian education is to open up communication between God and his people, the purpose comes to be fulfilled with boys and girls when they are led to see that Christianity is not an acceptance of certain facts, biblical or theological, but is rather an allegiance to a person, whose character is made known to us through biblical records.

Dr. Goldman has rightly said that the Bible is 'not a children's book', and he has inferred that there are many areas of its contents unsuitable for presentation to children. It should not be supposed, however, that this means the Bible has no place in Christian education programmes for children and boys and girls. This analysis of the needs of juniors and the selection of Bible material relevant to their needs shows that a great deal of the Bible can and should be brought to their knowledge. It can only be done, however, when the right means are chosen for the purpose, and when one is prepared to use Bible material, but not centre everything upon it. One cannot say too often that in the end it is the attitude of the teacher which matters most.

10

YOUNG PEOPLE

By the time boys and girls have moved into the period of adolescence they have begun to come to terms with life as a series of experiences within which personal decisions have to be made for which they themselves must be, to a large extent, personally responsible. The security of home life is still important to them, though they may be unaware of this, but their attitude to parental authority and responsibility has inevitably become quite different. Young people not only move out into life feeling independent; there is a sense in which they *are* independent. Moreover, the decisions to be made within their experiences no longer have a transient value; they acquire a heightened sense of finality and permanence which makes the recognition of consequence as important as motive.

By the time they have reached sixteen years of age many young people are compelled to make decisions about careers and employment which influence the whole of their future. Such decisions are often thrust upon them even when, 'scarcely knowing what they want to make of life, they are in danger of a false start, choosing, perhaps, some calling for which they have no real vocation or fitness, and thus intensifying ... their inner sense of uncertainty and insecurity'.[1]

By the time they have reached seventeen many of them have made, or are making, decisions about the choice of friends with a view to marriage and the

[1] B. A. Yeaxlee, op. cit.

establishing of a home life for themselves. The economic pressures leading to the choice of employment may be obvious to society; there has been less readiness to understand the psychological pressures exerted upon the young to enter into marriage.

It is during the same period that the challenge of the Christian faith takes on particular significance, whether accepted or deferred or rejected, for all that the faith means has particular relevance to their personal needs and circumstances, and cannot help but be related to the wider decisions in life which they are being compelled to make.

All of this is important to the Christian teacher, for it opens up channels of communication which have hitherto been closed, or only partially opened by the theoretic speculations about life on the part of younger boys and girls. It is not without significance that Harold Loukes found his most rewarding entry into the minds of young people by relating his religious instruction to such subjects as Friendship; Sex and Marriage; Money; Work; Leisure, etc.[1] And the Bible, properly understood, has still a great deal that is of value to tell us about these subjects. Indeed, one of the defects of the Sex and Morality Report[2] presented to the British Council of Churches is to be seen in its apparent unwillingness to explore Bible teaching at the level of experience and in terms of Bible theology on the grounds that a textual analysis of the subject was unsatisfactory.

It is also important because one assumes that the presentation of the Bible material will become increasingly related to the evoking of a response to Christ in personal terms during the period of adolescence. This assumption is not denied, for on every hand there is

[1] *Teenage Religion* by H. Loukes   (S. C. M.), 1961.
[2] *Sex and Morality* (S.C.M.), 1966.

ample evidence for its justification. And experience in adolescence that 'the self has passed from the state of being divided and consciously wrong, inferior and unhappy, to that of being unified and consciously right, superior and happy'[1] is one which some of us can recall ourselves, and which lies at the heart of true evangelism.

Nevertheless, one should also remember that such an experience is not, or ought not to be, an end in itself. There is a warning to be heeded, well described in the words of Professor Niblett, 'In some a vivid experience, necessarily partial, inhibits further spiritual development, leading to bigotry or to disillusion. In others, apparently the same experience, no less partial, is a gateway to growth.'[2] The Bible has also a great deal to teach us about the ways in which the resolution of tension ought to lead to further progress towards true maturity.

Behind these fundamental questions about life and its relationship, about decision-making and the consequences, lies the problem of the attitude of the young people to the Bible itself. One hopes that in time adolescence will be reached without an accretion of the wrong ideas about the Bible, but even so it is during the period of fourteen to twenty that the questions associated with the reliability and authority of the Bible are inevitably brought out into the open and have honestly to be faced.

However well parents and teachers have sought to answer the questions 'What?', 'Why?', 'How?', it is these same questions, but now at a new dimension of understanding and awareness, that are asked afresh in

---

[1] *Varieties of Religious Experience* by William James. (Fontana) 1960.

[2] *Christian Education in a Secular Society* by W. R. Niblett, (L.U.P.), 1960.

adolescence. Young people are no longer prepared to take for granted the word of parent or teacher, however much respected.

Authoritative answers, however wise and right for growing boys and girls, are no longer sufficient. They want to know for themselves. There is a pertinent comment on this, quoted by H. Loukes, from a member of his class. 'It's much better,' he said, 'to be able to sit and discuss the things that your teacher's telling you about than to just have to sit and listen, and think, oh well, if the teacher says "that's right" surely it must be so.'[1]

There is a genuine desire to know the truth for themselves, and it is a grave misunderstanding of the situation for teachers to become impatient with the incessant questions asked by young people. If they do query so much that seems to be beyond dispute it is not because they are 'blasé, disillusioned, impertinently self-satisfied, peevishly discontented, or thoughtlessly revolutionary'.[2] Rather is it a concern to discover at first-hand what is true and real, what is best, and what can really work in their lives.

It is necessary to state now that no attempt is made here to show how best the Bible and biblical material can be introduced to young people. The principles of the approach have been considered elsewhere, and quite clearly they will apply differently to different needs, as to the committed or the uncommitted, to those with above average intelligence and those less well equipped. But for all, two things are necessary.

Firstly, there must be the willingness to open up the whole subject of what the Bible is (and is not), why it has its place in the life of the Church and the Christian

[1] Op. cit.
[2] B. A. Yeaxlee, op. cit.

religion, and how it came to be written and handed down for us to use today. And, secondly, an attempt must be made to indicate its unity in Christ as the supreme revealer of God and his purpose for mankind, and the unified truths (or Bible theology) about God and man which emerge from a study of its pages.

To do these things effectively teachers must be sure in their minds about the purpose they are seeking to fulfil. There must be an openness of approach, a frank recognition of problems raised, an honest appraisal of the place of the Bible in the life of the Church; but there must be also an awareness of the need – when all discussion is ended – to re-establish the reliability and authority of the Bible. This must emerge, and not be imposed, but without such emergence the Christian teacher has not succeeded in his task.

Those who are responsible for teaching the Bible need perhaps to recognize that the intellectual environment in which they teach has changed remarkably during the past thirty years. There was a time when a supposedly 'modern' attitude to the Bible was 'liberating and illuminating against a background of fundamentalism and conservatism'.[1] Such a 'modern' attitude to dissection and analysis is not only no longer modern, it is also 'confusing or merely dull against a background of unbelief.'

The apparent readiness on the part of some young people to find security in fundamentalism needs to be understood rather than offensively attacked, particularly in a time of increasing secularism. The task of teachers is to show that such security is not to be found in an irrational acceptance of infallibility, but in a reasoned conception of reliability and authority.

Only by the serious tackling of the answers to the

[1] W. R. Niblett, op. cit.

'What?', 'Why?' and 'How?' concerning the Bible is it possible to bring cohesion to the fragments of Bible knowledge acquired in the years before adolescence. Certain facts will have been communicated to boys and girls in a review of the Bible, but it is only possible to bring a proper historical perspective to the facts when they have moved beyond the age of twelve. From then onwards young people have an increasing awareness of historical periods, and can begin to appreciate the spiritual development of the Hebrews, and the setting of Christ's incarnation in that development.

It is important to note, however, that we live in a time when the importance of history as a subject in its own right is underrated. The historical cohesion of Bible stories and situations must be related to the purpose for which the study is intended. At the same time there must be an emphasis upon the historicity of Jesus, not because this by itself may weigh heavily in favour of his acceptance, but because young people insist on knowing the facts. It is not an unimportant fact that the life of Christ has historic foundation.

In certain situations, young people are now more prepared to begin a study of the Bible in depth, not merely as illustrative, even if inspired, material to be put alongside parallel experiences in life, but as a study in its own right. There will be serious students, committed to examinations or to a desire to come to grips with the reality of the Bible message. There will be others who will need to be encouraged to look at one or other of the books in the Bible to see how what they have learned can be applied to such study.

One may take Mark's Gospel as a record of the life and teaching of Jesus Christ, and as the earliest of the Gospels in the Bible to be written. 1 Corinthians is an interesting example of the early Christian letters and offers a fund of material relevant to modern life, within the Church itself, and in society. Amos and Hosea are obvious choices for a study of the important era of prophecy in the eighth century B.C., as formative influences in Hebrew religion and foundations of Christian moral teaching.

It is during adolescence, too, that because of the studies discussed above, one can begin to indicate more positively the interplay of the parallelism of experience. If the habit has been established of looking at life and modern experience and then seeing what can be learned by putting similar biblical situations alongside, it is now that one can show more clearly how the opposite process may be followed.

The reading of Bible passages affords the opportunity to discover what elements in modern life are illustrated by those Bible passages. There is emancipation from a textual approach, with its glib and superficial acceptance of 'God's word'. In its place there is an understanding of the true word which God is speaking through and beneath the words, which is relevant to man's condition now. The Bible again begins to come into its own, and more are encouraged to read it and to search for the truth it contains. There is no blind acceptance of isolated texts; no imprisonment in verbalism; no 'sticking of pins' into the 'book' for God's guidance. Instead there can be developed an appreciation of the true guidance of the Holy Spirit as we seek the treasure that has at once been hidden and yet can so easily be revealed.

Text-books in adolescent psychology invariably point out that young people are seeking for a philosophy of life which makes sense to them. Just as the early years of childhood lay the foundations of emotional attitudes, so the years of youth lay the foundations of intellectual attitudes. These two poles of experience and understanding may be much more closely related than has been realized, and one cannot artificially separate feeling and thinking. Yet, whether aware of it or not, young people are indeed seeking to find a way of life that makes sense and gives them some kind of integrated philosophy. Some aspects of this have already been implied in what has been written in this chapter.

Within such a search a co-ordinated and coherent attitude to the Bible will be of profound significance. It is more important that young people be given a way of looking at the Bible, a way of studying the Bible, than a series of facts about the Bible. The more they are able to establish for themselves principles of judgment and interpretation, the more they will be able to apply those principles throughout their lives, and continue to be stimulated by Bible study. This may, of course, be effected in adulthood, but it will be more difficult then as attitudes, criteria of judgment, and built-in prejudices tend to harden. For Christian teachers, the period of life between fourteen and twenty is, humanly speaking, the last opportunity for influencing significantly those whom they wish to reach.

For this reason, the attitude of such teachers – as with the other age ranges – is of the utmost importance. With young people, the rôle of the leader or teacher must be 'to study the Bible with youth and not to indoctrinate them. The leader has to listen before he speaks. He is with the young people to help them listen instead of giving them a final and authoritative answer. ... He should be ready to cope with the seemingly irrelevant questions that the young people might raise.'[1]

It is wrong to indoctrinate at any age, and an overt authoritarianism will be resented by boys and girls even

[1] Hiroshi Shinmai, 'Learning to Interpret' in *World Christian Education*, Vol. XXI, No. 1, 1966.

if it seems at the time to be accepted. Young people are less willing to accept it, and it is right that they be given every encouragement to think things through for themselves. But it is still wrong, even when young people seem themselves eager to be given answers to their questions and want the security of an authority. Nothing stultifies spiritual growth more than a passive acceptance of that which is given, unless it be the emotional response to the personality of an authoritative teacher. The teacher may wish to guide in order to build up security; his personality is a factor in communication which has its proper place. But if young people are to mature, teachers need to understand the nature of their function, its limitation as well as its opportunity. Once they are clear about their function, and have the right attitude themselves to the Bible, we may see a break-through in the re-establishing of the Scriptures as literature which is understood, read, and appreciated.

11

ADULTS

ONE of the encouraging signs of the time is a revival of interest in Christian education among boys and girls and young people. The controversies and discussions; the research and experimentation; the evidences of failure and widespread dissatisfaction; all these are symptoms, not of despair, but of resolve to achieve better results in the future. And society, in education and in church life, continues to provide opportunities for Christian education for the benefit of those growing up in its midst. The Education Act of 1944 ensures that religious instruction in some form or other is given to the vast majority of boys and girls up to the age of fifteen, and among slightly less numbers beyond that. The life of most churches, where there is any life at all, is centred upon a strong programme of fellowship, instruction and recreation for those up to twenty years of age.

It must be said, however, that once the age of twenty has been passed, a very different picture presents itself. The overwhelming majority of members of adult communities are unaffected by educational facilities and indifferent to church fellowships. Christian education, and the place of the Bible within such education, seems able to reach only small numbers. And even among these, a consistent pattern of education and enlightened Bible study, is almost non-existent. For one reason or another, churches seem to have come to the position of relying almost entirely upon sermons within the context of worship for education, and upon Bible readings within the same context for the communication of Bible truth. Where adults meet in fellowships, groups, or church-sponsored organizations, the emphasis is often upon entertainment and inspirational talks, rather than a serious programme of education. There can be no doubt that one of the greatest challenges to modern church life is the need to rebuild into its structure a consistent pattern of learning, not merely for its own sake but also to ensure that its mission to the wider community can be articulate and intelligent.

We are not concerned here about the ways in which this might be achieved, but already there is some indication of a concern that it should be done. The emphasis on Family Worship is beginning to open up prospects of adult sessions of Christian education taking place at the same time as sessions arranged for children and young people. The growing awareness of the need for the training of laity in order that they may fulfil their proper functions in the worship and mission of the Church is encouraging the promotion of courses and conferences. Even the present discontent in work among the young is giving rise to the demands for more training by adults responsible for such work. Above all, the growing demands of young adults, themselves brought up in an atmosphere of discussion and involvement in education, for house groups and Church programmes that are not merely inspirational as 'listening shops', is inevitably challenging the Church to re-think its approach towards them.[1]

There is no wish here to depreciate the value of regular preaching. There is only the concern for a revival of true Christian fellowship in which the things of God are studied in depth and taken seriously. Granted this, by whatever means it is reached, one can

[1] cf. *Young Adults and the Church* (M.Y.D.), 1965.

I

begin to discuss the place of the Bible in such study.

One word of caution needs to be offered at the very beginning. Throughout this book an attempt has been made to show that teachers who regard the Bible as an end in itself are misusing it. The goal before us is wider than scriptural knowledge, and while there is a place for Bible-study in its own right, it retains its proper place only when that wider goal is always kept in sight. Among adults, there is a danger that their very commitment to Christ and eagerness to understand his truth may lead to an introverted study of the Bible, again for its own sake. When this happens, the fellowship group and its study of the Scriptures may become a way of escape from the challenges of life rather than a springboard into Christian involvement.

At the same time, one has to recognize that the ideal pattern of educational development in ideas about the Bible is far from being realized, and that many problems associated with the Scriptures remain in the minds of adults. Much that we have described in looking at work among boys and girls and young people has necessarily to be repeated with adult groups. The difficulties which arise in regard to Science and Religion, the reliability and authority of the Bible, and the interpretation of the Scriptures, often lie buried in the minds of adults. For some there has been an unwillingness to face the difficulties for fear that by so doing they may lose their faith or be disloyal to what they believe it to be. For others there has been an abandonment of the Bible as a book to be taken seriously. For all, therefore, there is value in setting out openly and clearly the difficulties which must be overcome if a genuine break-through in Bible-study is to be achieved.

In some cases, these difficulties may be dealt with as they arise; in other cases it may be necessary to run a short introductory course, setting the scene, and clearing away the more obvious difficulties, before proceeding. But at no time should there be evasion. It is easy and cheap to delude (even with the best motives) those who are committed to the Christian religion by snide references to the fallibility of science and emotive phrases about the Word of God within the closed setting of church fellowship. But apart from what we may think about intellectual integrity and the wholeness of truth, approaches of this kind only serve to make Christians helpless and bewildered when they seek to talk with the uncommitted about their faith and the Bible, which records the grounds upon which faith may rest.

We can now begin to examine the particular biblical emphases in reference to adult groups. And because one is dealing with adults whose experiences are wide, there are few, if any, themes about life which will not be of interest to them. Because, by their very presence in the group, they are committed in some way to Christ and his Church, they will be ready to learn what it means to be a 'covenanted people' or 'the people of God'. They will be concerned to study the various New Testament images of the Church. They will respond to the qualities of discipleship as revealed by the Scriptures.[1] Such studies are important, not only for the biblical insights they offer, but also for an appreciation of the heritage into which they have entered and an understanding of what they and their Church ought to be like in their own contemporary setting.

Wideness of experiences in life also enables a biblical study to be made of the central theological truths which express the Christian faith, and their own faith, in a co-ordinated fashion. Forgiveness and reconciliation;

[1] cf. *Christian Nurture and the Church* by R.C. Miller, (Scribners: New York).

suffering and sin; the nature of God and man, are but a few areas of Christian thought which are illuminated by the study of relevant Bible passages.

More detailed study of particular books of the Bible can well be limited to such themes as the 'Life and Ministry of Peter' (to which I personally have always found adults respond – he seems very near to the experiences of ordinary men and women!) and 'The Vision and Witness of Paul', alongside the more obvious ones of 'The Life and Teaching of our Lord', or 'The Meaning of the Kingdom of God'.

The study of themes such as these gives one the opportunity of looking in breadth and depth at subjects embedded in the Scriptures and yet very pertinent to the growth of the personal spiritual life and the problems which every person, sooner or later, has to encounter. And, again, the secret of it all is to avoid the temptation of giving superficial, textual answers to problems, but instead to promote ways of thinking and attitudes of mind.

It is perhaps asking for the impossible to assume that a total church membership will want to be involved in fellowship groups of this kind. However attractive and worthwhile we may believe them to be, there will always be those who do not respond. Moreover, we have to remember that there are usually those who belong to church life, but remain very much on the fringe of the spiritual life of the church. The kinds of approach which have to be made in Youth Club work can, however, be translated into the terms of adult group work. And while serious Bible-study may be out of the question, there is no reason why sessions, from time to time, should not be introduced which will help to promote a better understanding of the Bible.

Open Forums and Public Debate can also be

arranged, which may attract those who have strong views about the Bible and Religion, but who tend to assume that the Church's views are still the antiquated notions of the nineteenth century. Dr. Soper's experiences at Tower Hill and Hyde Park are an indication of a wide interest in religious matters, but a natural unwillingness to attend church to be lectured. Much more needs to be done to promote open encounter and discussion, preferably on neutral premises, in order that a wider adult constituency – whether on the fringe of church life or outside it – may become aware of an enlightened Christian interpretation of the faith, the Church and the Bible.

Reference was made earlier to sermons and selections of Bible passages in public worship as media for Christian education. This is not the place to consider the value of sermons, but a word does need to be said about Bible readings in corporate acts of worship. Not all denominations provide a church lectionary for the benefit of those who conduct worship, and in these cases one supposes that the leader of the worship will make suitable selections in accordance with the theme of the service. Some denominations provide a lectionary, but allow the ministers or preachers to exercise their own discretion as to whether or not they will use it. There are, however, others which provide a lectionary, and it is normally expected to be followed.

Such lectionaries have increasingly come under criticism in recent years. Certainly the intention that sooner or later every single chapter in the Bible ought to be read in an Order of Service, so that the whole of the Scriptures are eventually made known to regular worshippers, is lacking in imagination. It is by such a process that leaders of worship find themselves reading odd passages, particularly from the Old Testament, which are boring, incomprehensible or unsuitable as a part of worship. The perpetuation of schemes of reading of this kind is an insult to the people who are expected to participate in worship, and serves only to support the idea that the Church believes the Bible to be so different that its every word must carry inspirational value.

Perhaps as more churches become involved in a total strategy of Christian education, serious attention will be given to the selection of the passages of Scripture to be used in public worship, so that they may be co-ordinated with such a strategy. Congregations will quickly come to realize that such readings are related to the fellowship and group studies, and may respond more readily to the invitation to join them.

There is no reason, however, why Bible reading should not be prefaced by a short word of explanation or indication of theme, so that those who then listen to it can follow it more intelligently. Again, the growing practice of Family Worship, in which children have place, is encouraging this. But the needs of adults in this respect are often as great as the needs of the boys and girls themselves.

One other factor should be mentioned. As the need for active participation in learning processes becomes more widely recognized, so the promotion in the life of the Church of group discussions and Bible studies should be accompanied with suggestions for 'home-work' which adults would be expected to do from week to week. There is no reason why recommended passages of Scripture should not be read between meetings, either as prelude or sequel to the studies of the sessions. In those cases where corporate worship on Sunday is led normally by the same person, a similar process can be encouraged among the worshippers.

The acceptance of the idea that Christians are normally only to be exposed to the Word of God through sermons and perfunctory Bible readings can no longer be tolerated. It is nothing less than tragic that only fringe groups or strange sects should in the main still emphasize the fundamental need of Christians to know their Bible. There must be a restoration of confidence in the Bible, and a corresponding eagerness to receive its truth on the part of all Christians if they are to be equipped for the tasks to which God is calling them. An awakened concern to study the Scriptures has in every age been a natural accompaniment to revival and renewal. We have no reason to suppose that the twentieth century will be an exception.

12

THE BIBLE IN ART FORM

IT is imposssible adequately to survey the place of the Bible in Christian Education without reference to the variety of ways in which the arts have drawn inspiration from the Bible so that in turn they have helped people to understand something of its deeper meaning. No attempt has been made to apply this aspect of our study to the different age-ranges under review, but it needs to be said that, both as a background to the religious life and as a means of communicating specific ideas, the arts can profitably be introduced at every age.

The writings fo Marshall McLuhan, who has been described as a 'prophet of the present' are not easy to follow. His theory that 'the message is the medium'[1] has in turn received serious attention and suffered derision. One aspect of the theory is that the limitations of a one-dimension line of communication, such as hearing and speaking, have largely been overcome by multi-dimension lines of communications – involving instantaneously more than one of the senses. It is this new process, which is an extension of man himself in all his senses, possible in an age of electronics, world-wide radio and television, and mass-media of communication, which can radically affect the way in which the faith may be communicated.

For our purposes we need only remind ourselves that the 'imaging' of the Bible, by whatever medium, does

[1] *Understanding Media: The Extension of Man* by M. McLuhan (McGraw Hill), 1965.

lead to a greater involvement in the receiving of the message than when reliance is placed solely upon reading. Nevertheless, the Church in many areas of its life has been slow to recognize this, and only now is it beginning to receive the attention it deserves.

The first six centuries of Christianity were notable for the ways in which Bible material provided the basis of mural paintings in churches and chapels, and this continued to the Fall of the Roman Empire. There was a movement which sought to abolish this practice, called the Iconoclastic Controversy, but victory was achieved by the pro-image party, when, in 842, 'The religious value of representations in human forms of Christ, the Virgin, and the Saints were recognized'.[1] At a later period the Puritans had a more lasting effect in their opposition to art-forms of a religious character, and it is only now that Christianity in Britain is recovering from it.

During the Dark Ages, artistic illustrations of biblical themes were limited to the work of clerics, who continued to work on Bible manuscripts, and inserted within them carefully-designed and coloured representations of the text. The Renaissance brought about emancipation, and from then onwards artists of every school have been drawn to the Bible in a search for satisfying themes.

Apart from the classical paintings of biblical subjects, one should draw attention to the etchings of Blake[2] in the Romantic period, the expressionism of Roualt with his fiery mysticism,[3] and the psychological surrealist religious paintings of Salvador Dali,[4] since these not only form part of our cultural history, but in many ways

[1] Jean Keim in *Handbook of Western Painting* (Thames and Hudson).
[2] See, for example, *Satan smiting Job*.
[3] See, for example, *Head of Christ* or *Christ on the Sea of Galilee*.
[4] See, for example, *Christ of St. John on the Cross*.

can be referred to in courses of Christian education with telling effect.

The influence of the Bible is equally strong in the realm of music. Professor D. J. Grout has gone so far as to say that the 'history of western art begins with the music of the Christian Church'.[1] The chanting of psalms, the development of ancient hymns and canticles, the emergence of sung liturgies, all these helped to lay the foundations of Christian worship associated with Scripture and music.

Few serious composers have failed to make their contributions to the writing of Masses and Passion Stories, and the oratorios of Handel and others are embedded in the culture of English-speaking peoples. Eighteenth-century England might not know the Italian language, so that operatic performances could have comparatively little appeal, but its sturdy Protestantism meant that it did know the Old Testament. And there was a ready response to such works as 'Saul', 'Judas Maccabaeus' and 'Messiah'.

The twentieth century shows no lack of response to the Bible. Schoenberg's 'Moses and Aaron', Stravinsky's 'Symphony of Psalms' ('a masterpiece of invention, musical architecture, and religious devotion,'[2]) William Walton's 'Belshazzar's Feast' and Benjamin Britten's 'Noye's Fludde' are obvious examples.

If paintings and drawings have their use in Christian education, so does music. Much more imaginative use can be made of it, particularly in an age of tape recorders, record players and amplifying systems, and the playing of excerpts, carefully chosen, often proves a gateway to biblical truth that is not opened in any other way.

[1] D. J. Grout, *A History of Western Music* (Dent and Sons), 1960.
[2] D. J. Grout, op. cit.

The literary merit of the Bible has long been taken for granted, and there is no doubt that certain passages 'speak for themselves'. We know that in the last resort it is what the Bible means that matters most, with its clear testimony to the attributes and reality of God in his dealings with men. But one should not underrate the Bible 'designed to be read as literature'. There are those who are willing to acknowledge that the deepening of their spiritual life sprang first from an attraction to the Bible on its literary merits.

Recent recordings of Bible passages and stories by well-known actors and actresses again provide opportunities for the teacher to introduce such material in the best possible way.

So, as a background to cultural inspiration, and as a means of specific education, the art forms of paintings and drawings, of music, of drama and literature – all associated with biblical themes – can have their proper place in the stimulation of imagination, in the stirring of the soul, in the quickening of the mind.

When we have all done our best, or our worst, the Bible will still remain supreme and unique. As in the past, so now, with the ebb and flow of fashion, men will find here an inexhaustible source of illumination, guidance and faith.

The art form of film-making has so far proved least satisfying, and one must in truth say that biblical themes translated into the terms of the cinema have shown little imagination. They have often helped to preserve a literalism which can prove in the long run to be most dangerous. An attempt to produce a film which reflects the inner experiences and interpretation of events as men have sought to comprehend God's revelation, has yet to be made. Perhaps the nearest to this was the B.B.C. Television Series based on Christ's

Ministry, but this was produced for television itself, and not for the 'big screen'.

Reference ought also to be made to dramatic presentations of biblical themes, and in this sphere Dorothy Sayer's broadcast series of plays, entitled 'The Man Born to be King' is worth special mention. Attention should also be drawn to the combination of contemporary music and drama in terms of teenage culture exemplified in 'A Man Dies'. Perhaps we are on the fringe of a break-through in which a combination of film-making, music and drama, in genuine twentieth-century terms, will express the experiential approach to the great biblical themes waiting to be used.

And here the lines to be drawn between education and evangelism necessarily become blurred and indistinct. The twentieth century has rendered it almost impossible to communicate the faith, in education and in evangelism, in verbal communication alone. A multi-dimensional approach, using art forms, ancient and modern, is now almost essential to reach the multitudes effectively and relevantly.

For over a hundred years the meat of the Scriptures has been torn away so that for many all that is left is a kind of skeleton. The dry bones may seem to be of interest to the few specialists. The rest of the world assumes them to be just dry bones. But given a proper understanding of their nature, a right approach to their interpretation, and a willingness to use all means of communication and expression, the Holy Spirit will re-clothe these bones with living flesh; they will re-form and will live again. Man can and will discover that beneath the words of the Bible itself is to be found the living Word, and as he finds that living Word he himself will be given fulness of life.

SCRIPTURE REFERENCES

OLD TESTAMENT

NEW TESTAMENT

INDEX

143